V. Nicholas Gerasimou

Get up and Walk: A Stroll With Jesus

A Collection of Bite-Sized Essays About God:

V. Nicholas Gerasimou

Unless otherwise indicated, Bible quotations are taken from the NIV (New International Version) of the Bible

ISBN-10: 0615774329
ISBN-13: 978-0615774329

DEDICATION

This is for my boys. I thank God every day for giving you two to me. I pray one day you'll read this and understand your crazy old Dad a little better. I love you.

.

"In his heart a man plans his course, but the Lord determines his steps."

(Proverbs: 16-9)

V. Nicholas Gerasimou

CONTENTS

ACKNOWLEDGMENTS

First and foremost I want to give credit and thanks to my Lord Jesus. This book, nor anything else would have been possible without Him. I pray it glorifies Him in some small way.

To everyone who has given a little piece of yourself to me. Some of you still love me, some of you can't stand me, and some of you don't even know who you are. Such is life. I pray that one day we will all meet each other with new eyes and embrace in The Kingdom. Regardless, thanks for adding to my story. I hope I added a little something to yours.

To my good friend Dylan Cole; thank you for creating such amazing cover artwork for me. You are truly gifted.

V. Nicholas Gerasimou

V. Nicholas Gerasimou

CHAPTER ONE

*T*IMING IS EVERYTHING

Proverbs 16:9

In his heart, a man plots his course, but The Lord determines his
steps.

When I was nine years old, I remember my parents taking
my younger brother and I to Disneyland. We lived in Laguna
Niguel, and The Magic Kingdom was twenty-seven miles up
the 5 Freeway. Twenty-seven miles: may as well have been a
million. To my little nine-year-old brain, Mickey Mouse was on
the other side of the world, never to be hugged or high-fived.
Then, to add insult-to-injury you must understand that driving
in Southern California is not measured in distance. It's
measured in time. Precious, precious, time.

Southern California sprawls across roughly 56,000 square miles of over-priced real estate, and packed into that tiny pocket of bliss are just over 24 *MILLION* people. 24 Million people all trying to merge onto the 405 at rush hour. To put that in contrast, our hot, dry neighbor to the East, Arizona boasts 113,998 square miles of elbow room making it the sixth largest state in our union. Only 7.5 million people live there. We have over Three-Times the people crammed into an area over half as small. If someone asks you how far away something is and you answer with, "*10 miles*" you will most-likely be met with a blank stare and confusion. It's not *ten-miles* away, its *thirty-five minutes* away. But be sure to take the Toll-Road after 1:45pm because the 91 Eastbound is an absolute parking-lot heading into Riverside in the afternoon.

Disneyland was Twenty-seven miles away, but I swear as I sat in that backseat with my forehead mashed against the window, looking at the olive-green Datsun putting along next to us, I was positive I would be buried in our car. As my Dad white-knuckled the steering wheel, trying his best to stay calm as I whined out the same question I'd asked seventeen times previous over the last eleven minutes, "*How-Much-Lonnnnggggeerrrrrrrrr-ahhhhhhhhh?*" He would respond through clenched teeth, "Soon. Same as it was the last time you asked. Just relax and enjoy the ride, son."

Enjoy the ride. Enjoy-the-ride? Had the old-man lost his mind? He was forty-five after-all. To nine-year-old me he must have been born sometime after the late Cretaceous Period. The ride was torture. The ride was eternal. The ride… was fifty-five minutes. It's just that to my pre-pubescent brain, the entire concept of time was abstract. I lacked a few things which would have allowed me to endure the ride in relative peace and tranquility.

First, I didn't really have a pre-frontal-cortex worth talking about. My Amygdala was still wet clay and my definitions of logic and sense were derived from countless hours spent watching Saturday-Morning-Cartoons. Second, I was nine. I hadn't been on Earth long enough to earn perspective. I hadn't lived through my teens; Or middle-school; Or high school algebra, yet. I didn't understand that the way we experience time is relative to the individual person experiencing it. Time flies when you're having fun, but grinds to a sloth stuck in quicksand, snail's-pace when you're bored.

The same way I lacked the perspective to see that, of-course - my Dad was right and we would make it to the land of the over-priced hotdog and two-hour ride wait times, we lack the perspective to see that God's plan is perfect on the Macro level. We only see the tiny sliver of time we exist in. Minute by minute, moment by moment, we experience time as linear and unknown. God sees it a bit differently. He sees it all at once, beginning, middle, and end. What is thirty-five years on Earth compared to an eternity outside of time? We have no hope of seeing time for what it is. To God we are all whiny kids buckled into our boosters in the backseat, sing-song whining about how long the drive is.

Speaking of time, this book represents over two decades of my life. I started to write it as a sort of a personal journal and over the decades it kind-of metastasized into a novel…who knew? When I began to put it all together, I was sure that it would be finished in a year. I was positive of it. The Lord obviously had other plans for it…for me. At the time ("the time" being every day over the past decade) I questioned why?

I would promise myself that, "This summer I'm gonna' hunker down and write like I've never written before, this time's going to be different," then just like every other bold promise I'd proclaimed to myself, life jumped up and called it out, told it to meet behind the gymnasium at 3:00pm sharp to rumble, and proceeded to beat it back into the shadows of my mind; like a vampire, arms crossed in front of its face reluctantly retreating from the morning sun.

This collection of essays has seen over twenty years, five jobs, six cities and three apartments. It's been through five relationships, one house, true love, heart break, a marriage, divorce, one very, very good dog, my two amazing children, extreme joys, midnight depressions and periods of backsliding.

This book has seen the dark dusty inside of a drawer for months at a time as I left it to rust, and it has seen periods of closeness with Jesus that I have yet to duplicate. It's been the recipient of frenzied periods of manic attention accompanied by stretches of insomnia to provide the time, and been the cause of such mind-numbing mental blockage that was so thick I had trouble articulating normal everyday conversation afterward (can I have one of those…uhh…things…you know…uhh…two pieces of bread, meat, cheese, lettuce, mustard…oh you know what I mean).

It has seen pain: emotional, spiritual and physical. It's seen me hurt by others and watched as I did the hurting. It has seen much of the bad I do, the sin, the weakness…as well as the good. The question is why? Why so much? Why so long?

I think The Lord needed me to experience life a bit more for me to truly be able to do this work justice. He needed me to grow. He needed me to walk with Him. He had things to show me. Just as He may have things to show you. It's easy to trick yourself into thinking you're too busy to listen when the Lord calls your name. I just have too many things on my plate right now to stop what I'm doing and go for a walk with the Lord. Don't make that mistake. Listen. Heed His call. Take a stroll.

I guarantee you that The Lord's timing is always perfect. Even though it may not always seem that way to you. He's never late and He's never early. He…is. He's there exactly when you need Him, at the exact moment you need Him there. Always.

As for me, I finally feel that The Lord is telling me that the timing is right. If this book helps just one of you who read it gain a better understanding of Jesus, or somehow helps draw you closer to The Lord, or if it just brings a smile to your face for a moment and makes you laugh…then I feel that it's done its job.

As an aside, God has a sense of humor. With two young boys under ten, car rides can be a challenge. To me, the drive to Anaheim to visit the land of giant cartoon rodents and water fowl, with the radio on, windows down is a thirty-minute vacation from the stress in my life. Sips of coffee, intercut with the solitude of my own little kingdom of silence. That is until two whining banshees start wailing the laments of endless car-rides, eternal traffic, and that we have in-fact, been in the automobile… for-ev-er, from the back seat.

As I white knuckle the steering wheel, and shoot replies behind me through clenched teeth, I can't help but smile a bit at the irony of my situation, and the grace God affords us to gain perspective, before He turns the car around. We'll get there soon.

Good reading all, and God Bless!

V. Nicholas Gerasimou

CHAPTER TWO

COME TAKE A WALK WITH ME

Micah 6:8

[T]he Lord has told you what is good, and this is what He requires of
you: to do what is right, to love mercy, and to walk humbly with your
God.

The standard default blink-rate for the cursor of a
Microsoft WORD document is once every 530 milliseconds. It
just flashes, and flashes, and flashes. Taunting you. If you stare
at it long enough it almost becomes hypnotic. I say this
because that is exactly what I've been doing for the last hour-
and-a-half. Blink-Blink-Blink-Blink… You-Have-Nothing-
Interesting-To-Say… Blink-Blink-Blink… Writers-Block-Can-
Become-Permanent. Shut up, stupid cursor!

Right now, I'm sure of few things. One, my back hurts. A lot. Two, I'd love a glass of water but the kitchen seems like it's in a different time-zone. Three, I could really use a walk. I twist in my chair and a chorus line of vertebra snap-crackle-and pop up my spine. Actually, a walk sounds great. Some fresh air. Envision it. You stand up…stretch, roll your head around to loosen your neck and reach for the door. As you pull on the handle cool, clean air rushes over you. You inhale and feel the crisp pine-scented breeze fill your lungs. One step and you're outside. You take a couple of short strides into the night, and the weight of the day slips off of your shoulders like it's tethered to the house. For a time, you are free. Free from stress, free from worry…free, from writer's block.

Walks are great. They're a kind of escape. You should see the sheer, unbridled joy that simple four-lettered word elicits in my Golden-Lab, Alex. You'd think I promised to line the streets with Porterhouse steaks. But there's more to it than that. When you think of a walk you typically picture yourself strolling down a quiet neighborhood street after a big holiday meal, or sauntering under the stars hand in hand with the one you love on a brisk moonlit night. The Webster's New-World Dictionary defines the word "walk" in two ways: first, "*To advance by moving the feet*," and second (and most important to my point) "*A person's usual mode of behavior.*"

A walk can be used to describe how you live your life. It is a present tense verb. It's in motion. As you live and breathe, go about your daily routine and interact with the world, you are walking through your life. Depending on the translation you use, the word for *walk* is used in the Bible over 315 times. But it's the context that is the most important. Many times, the word is used to describe a man's way of life, or his moral compass and value set. Ezekiel 11:20 says, "*He may walk as a carnal or as a spiritual man.* (NIV)" The King James Bible says in Romans 8:1, "*There is therefore now no condemnation to them which are in Christ Jesus, who walk not after the flesh, but after the Spirit.*" The Apostle John put it this way in 1 John 1: 5-7:

> If we claim to have fellowship with [H]im yet walk in the darkness, we lie and do not live by the truth. But if we walk in the light, as [H]e is in the light, we have fellowship with one another, and the blood of Jesus, [H]is son purifies us from all sin.

Is John actually talking about walking blindly through a dark room, groping around the wall by the door jam, flipping the switch, and then trotting around bathed in the soft yellow glow of a 100-watt bulb? Not likely. He's speaking of a relationship with God. Our relationship with God. Walking with Jesus. He's talking about living by His will. Remember, a person's usual mode of behavior.

I say all of this to introduce the premise of this collection of essays. Like I said earlier in my treatise on time, this book is an amalgamation of my ponderings, studies, laments, and experiences about-with-and-to, God. It is a work in progress, as is my relationship with The Lord.

A key point to take away from this chapter is the idea that when you go for a walk with someone, you have made the decision to spend intimate, one-on-one time with them. There are very few distractions on a walk. Typically, you are within arm's reach of your partner. You walk as equals, side-by-side. You share things that have been on your mind, or that have been weighing heavy on your heart. You laugh. You vent. You experience the world together. You both take in the beauty and stillness of nature, the sprawl of suburban master-planned tract neighborhoods, or gawk in awe at the massive man-made towers of a big city. And if someone is faster or slower than you are, you begin to match their pace. You walk with them.

A question I've had to ask myself countless times over my life is: Am I walking with Jesus right now? Am I taking the time to direct my attention and focus completely onto Him? Am I living by His will and teachings? If I'm being honest, there have been a good number of times where my answer is no. I've had a meal with Jesus (realistically I've had a rushed 10 second prayer before I eat *at* Him). I've had a spot in between songs, in the car with Jesus. Sometimes I can fit in a quick chat with God while I brush my teeth before I get side-tracked and pick up with my hectic day.

All this to say, many times I prioritize Him last on my list of "To-Do's". It's not like He's going anywhere, right? He's eternal. He understands. It's usually during those times, where my time allocation is skewed, and I'm walking in the world instead of with God, that my life always starts to fall apart. My relationships sour, my mental health nosedives, and joy and peace seem to be in short supply. I struggle. I stumble. I fall. Then once I'm on my back I look up and see My Lord. It's Jesus, smiling. He extends a hand and asks if I'd like to go for a walk with Him. To spend some time, just the two of us.

I take his hand and get to my feet, dust myself off, and we step outside... together. I follow and take a couple of short strides into the night. I feel the release as the weight of the day slips off of my weary back and humbly watch as Jesus reaches out, takes my burdens, my stress, and my sin, and slides it over His shoulder's to carry it for me. It doesn't seem to faze Him. He motions for me to follow and we start to walk, side-by-side. Amazingly it's only after those moments, when I refocus on God that the puzzle-pieces of my life seem to slide back together.

It may very-well be the same for you. So, let's set down our "*all important*" lives for a bit, stretch, and take a stroll with Jesus. You look like you could use a walk.

CHAPTER THREE

*T*HE LEARNING PROCESS
Psalm 25:5

Guide me in your truth and teach me, for you are God my Savior,
and my hope is in you all day long.

I've coached high school sports for over two-decades.
Football, Track-&-Field, and Olympic Lifting. Uncoordinated
Freshmen, to top-tier Division-1 bound superstars. One thing
that never changes are the fundamentals. Speed and technique
are built on the simple pillars of foot placement, body
mechanics, and kinetic energy optimization. I can watch an
athlete run, hurdle, tackle, or preform a lift and immediately
see micro adjustments they need to make to improve their
speed, strength, or flexibility.

I say all of this to let you know that I have an eye for this
stuff and I *personally* feel that I'm qualified to speak on these

matters with some authority. A few years ago, my sons both began their own athletic careers. The joys of bee-hive soccer and rugby-basketball (where dribbling is optional). I loved coaching them as goofy toddlers and watching them develop a love for competing. As they've matured they've become more adept at their sports and details have started to matter.

Now, technique and precision have come into play. Natural ability is starting to be balanced out by coaching and intelligence. My youngest son Lincoln, needs to fix his running form. He's fast, but currently when he is at top speed he looks uncannily like one of those giant inflatable gyrating stick-men, planted outside one of your local used car dealerships. There's a lot of wasted movement.

Watching him sprint towards me, face locked in a grimace of effort, my mind shoots back to when he was just learning to walk. Toddlers have enormous heads in proportion to their bodies. It's like a watermelon stuck on top of a toothpick. My young Link was no exception. He actually seemed to be more top-heavy than most. I remember him standing for the first time, then taking a wobbly jerking step, and then working up to his first solo trip across the living room. But in between those events there were a countless number of, let's call them recalibrations.

There were times when he would just go head over heels in whichever direction his head tilted. One second, he's smiling at you, the next he's looking up at you from the floor wondering what happened. If he got going any one way too quickly, the inertia from his oversized cranium would carry him away until he got going faster than his little uncoordinated feet could keep pace.

I can't tell you how many walls, tables, chairs, sliding glass windows (pretty much anything about the height of my knee) that I was witness to the poor boy bouncing off of. The learning process was slow. Sometimes painfully so. I can attest to the buckets of tears I saw my little Lincoln spill. What Lincoln didn't know was that he was never alone. I was always there. I would hover over him with my arms at-the-ready. I'd crawl just behind him to keep him from any real injury. When he fell I would pick him up, plop him back on his chubby feet, and set him off on his waddling way again. No panic, no fretting, just a quick pat on the backside and smile. "Let's try again."

It's a long process. Lincoln looked to me for guidance. He looked to me protection, encouragement, and validation. He still does. I see my young son and I know exactly what he's feeling because I've been there. I can empathize with him. Did I expect him to take step after graceful step right away? Of course not. I remember what it felt like to learn. The frustration. The pain of failure. The uncertainness of letting go of Mom's hands and crossing the void all by yourself to Dad's outstretched arms. I knew he had the desire to walk. I knew he had the will to walk. He just didn't have the muscle coordination or strength to do it right away. Did I fault him for it? No. He's just a child. I knew that it was going to take a long time for him to learn. I knew that and welcomed it. That's part of the joy of watching a child grow.

I see a number of parallels in our walk with Jesus. When we start our relationship with God and make the decision to follow Him, what changes about us? How do we differ from the "*Old Us*" we once were? I would love to say that when I realized that Jesus was my savior and accepted Him into my life, I was instantly changed and was a shining example to the world on how to live by Christian principles. I'd love to say that, but it'd be a lie. I accepted Jesus and… not much changed at first. I was still a sinner (still am). I still did things, said things, and thought things that were completely contrary to what Jesus wanted me to do.

I had no idea how to follow Christ. All I knew was that now when I did, and said, and thought those things, I felt guilty afterward. I knew that I needed forgiveness. I was acutely aware of my own brokenness. That didn't change the fact that I was still broken. I needed to heal and healing takes time. I had to learn how to make better choices. I had to learn how to refocus on Jesus when the world clouded my vison. I had to learn how to be honest with myself and with humility ask Jesus for help and grace. The leaning process was slow. Painfully so.

I still fall. I still stumble. I'll get going one way too quickly and my big stupid head will carry me into a wall. I'll bounce off a table leg. Or more realistically I'll slip into a sin. Anger will hijack my brain while I'm stuck in traffic and frustration will fly out of my mouth. I still have moments of jealousy. Of greed. Of lust. Of all of the attributes that this fallen sinful body has to offer.

My walk with the Lord has been a struggle at times and at others it has been an all-out fight. When Lincoln would get frustrated and throw a tantrum I would just chuckle to myself. He'd look up at me with his little round, red face, tears streaming down the sides of his cheeks, upset that he couldn't do what he wanted to do. He wanted to walk so badly.

I would pick him up, give him a hug, tell him he was doing great, and we'd start again. The Lord does the same for us when we fall. Lincoln is nine now and in need of some correction on his running form. Not much has changed in how he reacts to my correction. I can see what he needs to change.

In real time I can call out how to change his elbow placement, the internal rotation of his toes, and how much he is crossing his midline with his arm thus wasting kinetic energy that should be thrown forward. He reacts much the same as he did as a one-year-old learning to walk. He throws back his head and scoffs. He gets frustrated. Dejected. Angry at himself, and then by-proxy, me for correcting him. I just smile. He'll get it eventually.

I still struggle with letting go. Letting go of my pride. My IN-DE-PEN-DENCE. Sometimes I still think I can do it on my own. Or maybe I'll just give God a little break and handle this one for Him. You know, it's the least I could do. Then my big head tilts to one side and, "Boom" there I go into a wall. "Bang" I bounce off a door-jam. I fall and pout, and wonder how I got there. It's only when I look up again and see the outstretched hand of the Lord that I come back to myself. "Sorry Lord," I say as I hang my head in shame. "I did it again. I just thought…" Well there I go thinking again.

When the Lord speaks, He speaks to your heart. "*You are forgiven my child. Rely on me. I love you.*" So, take His hand, accept His help, embrace His love. Realize that He doesn't expect you to do it alone. He wants you to walk with Him. The learning process is slow. Let Him teach you how.

CHAPTER FOUR

*T*HE BIG PICTURE

Psalm 73:24

"You will guide me with Your counsel, and afterward receive me to glory."

I was looking at a picture of myself the other day. It's a good picture. Not just of me, but as a whole it's a good picture. It's of a night I had on my last birthday. My younger brother Dean, and Adrian one of my closest and oldest friends took me out to eat. Like I said, it's a good picture. I am in the middle, Dean is to my left, and Adrian is to my right.

We all look happy. Smiles all around. Eyes beaming, teeth shining. It represents a happy night. But at times I can tend to be a bit particular. A little bit nit-picky if you will.

I just started to look at the picture. I really looked. I am one of those people who are hit or miss in photographs. I either look pretty good or like a train-wreck. There is no middle ground. I thought at first that I had lucked out. I thought that the planets had aligned and I had recorded a decent picture.

But then I noticed. My ears are uneven (making my sideburns matchup is an exercise in frustration), the left side of my mouth tweaks down when I smile, and when I put on a little weight it goes straight to my face and my jaw-line melts away. How had I not noticed at first? I got hit from the wrong angle. All three. It was a tri-fecta of photographic disaster. And where in the world did all of those lines around my eyes come from? Were those gray hairs!?

So I looked harder, closer. My teeth really aren't as white as I thought they were, and *wow* neither are Dean's. My hair is actually smashed down a bit on the left side of my head and now that we're talking, the pores on my nose looked so big that I probably could have dropped bowling balls into each one with room left over.

What in the world was I thinking? I am hideous and that is a horrible photo. It should be shredded, burned and the ashes should be locked in a lead box and dropped to the bottom of the Marianas Trench never to be seen again.

Afterward I should be banned from ever being in front a working camera. It was at that moment, at the height of my hysteria (when I was about to start working my way back through some of my old albums, looking to confirm my new revelation) that my brother walked into the room and made an offhand comment about what a fun night that was.

I begrudgingly agreed with him and then turned my attention back to the photo. I took a deep breath, rubbed my eyes and looked again. It *was* a happy picture. A great night. It was a time that I was able to spend time with people I care about; people who care about me. I sat there and lost sight of the big picture. I let pride take over. I let vanity cloud my vision and ruin an amazing memory.

The big picture. The big, big picture. What exactly is the big picture? Is it that we will eventually get *the* job? Is it that we will eventually get the *recognition* that we deserve? Will I eventually get into heaven? Do we just have to be patient? Calm? Persistent? *"Well I've prayed. I've talked to God about it. Have I talked enough? Have I talked too much?"* What *is* the big picture? What do we really want out of life? Fame, fortune, glory, peace, happiness…salvation?

Well, if you think about it, our lives are kind of like a

photograph to God. We are merely a snapshot in time to the Lord. How long can our (on average) 80 years really seem when you've been around for…ever? God sees us as a whole. He can see the beginning, middle and end of our lives at the same time. To Him, our short mortal life is like looking at a photo of a loved one who will be coming home soon. He can see the whole picture.

I imagine God as a patient parent sitting at a breakfast nook on a warm spring morning. He is sipping His coffee and flipping through a stack of photos that He has sitting on the table before Him. As He sits and takes in each new photo, waves of emotion wash over His face. Joy, adoration, pride, thoughtfulness, longing, and let's not kid ourselves…pain.

I always see myself as an annoying four year old (although I'm sure that there are those who would tell you that that description isn't far off) who hops up to the table, eyes and nose just barely peeping over the top. I ask God what He's doing and He tells me that He's looking at pictures of the most important person in the world. I ask who? He spins the package around with a finger and tells me to read the name on the cover.

I scramble up next to Him and look over His shoulder. The package has *my* name on it. My eyes pop open like dinner plates, a ring of surprise where my mouth should be. "*Me?*" I ask with a thumb in my chest. The Lord says "Who else?" I motion to Him with quick flaps of my hands to see one, so He hands me a picture.

I am honored. Beside myself with glee. God thinks *I* am the most important person in the world and wants to share pictures that He's taken of me.

I look. I pull my face back, a look of confusion and incomprehension twisting my features. I look at the picture, back at God, at the picture, back at God. Finally I shake my head. "I think your camera was out of focus," I say. The Lord simply smiles and tells me to look harder. So I look. Everything is blurred. The colors are smeared into one another and I can only make out vague objects. A hand here, an ear there. "*I don't understand,*" I say, "*This is so ugly, distorted. I look like a monster.*"

The Lord pats me on the back and tells me that it's because I'm not seeing the big picture. The big picture? Well okay, I must have to look at it from farther away…maybe then. So before the Lord can say anything else I set the photo down and run to the far end of the room.

Nothing.

So I run down the hall and into the bedroom.

Still blurry and now it's getting hard to see. God just smiles and chuckles a bit to Himself. How foolish can we be? But I keep trying. I want to see what God sees. I take the picture from God, run out the front door, put the picture in the middle of the street and trot down a block.

Nothing.

Two blocks…Nada.

I still can't see the big picture.

I am desperate to see the big picture and I am convinced that I can see it for myself.

I climb to the top of the highest water tower in town and peer over the edge toward my neighborhood, teetering on my tip-toes to try to catch a glimpse of how God sees me.

All I see is haze.

I slump down the railing and plop on my rear…elbows resting on my knees, head hung in defeat.

How far do I have to go? How big do I have to be to see what God sees? What am I doing wrong?

"Nothing."

I raise my head to see that God is sitting beside me.

"How did you get here so fast?" I ask. He simply smiles and tells me that He's always with me. He says that He was actually standing next to me the whole time but I was just too busy to notice. I nod, barely hearing, then quickly ramble through my recent exploits and whine about my failed attempts to see the big picture. God tells me that He already knows. I mumble an acknowledgement, only thinking about what I want to say next to the Lord. Then I start to rev-up again and chatter about my newest ideas on how to accomplish my goal. The Lord quiets me with a look.

I tend to get lost easily. Not in the driving in circles sense, but in the, *"Why am I here?"*, *"What is my purpose?"* sense. I am constantly trying to see the big picture. The only problem is that the only one big enough to see the big picture…is God. I always try to steal His thunder so to speak. The big picture. I looked at the picture of my birthday night and got caught up in the little details which were insignificant to the grand scheme. Like I said earlier, I let the earthly desires taint my view. Pride, vanity, greed to name a few. I couldn't see the forest through the trees, if I may use the cliché.

Let's step back and look if we can see a little more, shall we? What is the big picture of life? Is this world and all of the earthly desires, and possessions, and accomplishments…*if?* Is *this* what we're working for? I certainly hope not.

The big picture is eternity folks. I don't pretend to know what eternity will be like. I haven't the slightest clue. I know what the Bible tells us about it, that's it. I get caught up in the day to day of life like most of us. Money, cars, a new 75-inch flat-screen plasma HD integrated 3D digital TV…whatever. It's hard to sit down, open the Bible and read while simultaneously learning, growing, and praying…all while your checkbook is sitting on the coffee table taunting you with it's *unbalancedness*, your boss is doubling your work load, and you haven't slept in three nights because your downstairs neighbor has begun to host a nightly karaoke extravaganza in the room directly below your bed. At times quiet contemplation can be hard to come by. I know it is for me. But what is truly more important?

My point is, does the money in my bank account equal happiness? Does God care about my truck? If the big picture is eternity with Jesus, then how intensely should we dwell on our (at best) 80 years *here*?

The big picture is eternal. That being said it would make sense that we need to have eternal minds. This is much more easily said than done. We are finite beings. God made us with an expiration date. To us everything has a beginning, middle and end. The concept of eternity, or infinity, or forever is incomprehensible to our time-driven, finite, human brains. The fact that God always was, is, and will always be is a hard one to wrap our minds around. Add on top of that the fact that He wants to spend eternity with *us*. At times it's hard for us to act accordingly. We need to think beyond our "things" and "titles" and "(you fill in the blank)". We need to constantly refocus on God.

The best way I can describe my faith is like a telescope with a busted O-ring. If I concentrate and constantly focus on God I can see Him. It's when I turn my attention away from Him and onto other worldly things that I lose sight. The lens slips out of focus and God becomes fuzzy, far away. My sightline, much like my relationship with God, needs constant attention.

So let's go back to the water tower. There I am, sitting next to God, frustrated and depressed that *I…I, I* can't see what God sees. I can't see the big picture. He leans over, puts an arm around my shoulder and pulls the picture out of His pocket (assuming He has pockets). He holds the picture up and tells me to look. So I look. Same picture, distorted, fuzzy, and ugly. Then He asks me if I trust Him. "Of course…I love you," I say. Then He says if I trust Him so much, why do I insist on doing everything apart from Him on my own? I open my mouth to speak then shut it dumbstruck. I have no answer.

There is no way that I can see myself as God sees me. I can't see the big picture of my life. I'm not big enough and most importantly…I'm not God. The only way I have any hope of even catching a glimpse of His plan or "the big picture" is to trust in Him completely. Seek His guidance and let Him show me the way. In a sense, to see the big picture through His eyes.

So He holds out the picture again. I sit, arms crossed, bottom lip pushed out in defiance, pouting with all of the gusto that a four-year-old can muster. He asks me to trust Him. I soften and inch closer to His side. He tells me to look, only this time He guides me on where and how to look at it. He tells me the secrets and turns it just right so that all of the colors come into focus. Slowly it becomes clearer. I can start to make out people…shapes…features. My eyes widen with glee. The Lord just smiles and pats me on the head. I can see it now. It's clear.

The pictures' of me, only I'm much older. I am leaning against a counter with a couple of other people. One of them looks a lot like my little brother, and the other person must know me because they have their arm around me. We are all beaming. Bright eyes, shining teeth, and joy in our faces.

It's a good picture. Looks like a happy night.

CHAPTER FIVE

*T*HE LONG LINE

Matthew 19: 30

But many who are first will be last, and many who are last will be first.

———————————

Sitting in traffic affords me the opportunity to do quite a few things. It gives me time to think. It gives me a chance to catch up on podcasts I've gotten behind on. It lets me slowly craft, intensify, and then simmer in an ocean of white-hot rage that raises my blood pressure and hits play on a macabre playlist of profane Mad-Lib expletives I'd like to yell at my fellow motorists that aren't driving like I think they should be. I like to have fun.

The high school I work at is built into a small canyon. It's a beautiful campus. Surrounded on three sides by rural chaparral and majestic rolling hills, the view is breathtaking. The only problem is that there is only one way in, and one way out. One two-lane road serves as the main and only artery to the school. Well, our school has high, Car-lestorol. Get it? Artery? Car... lesterol?

Due to that logjam of humanity every morning, getting onto campus can be a time-consuming task. But, while I wait... I wait. I do my duty. I follow the rules. I look at it like, if everyone follows the rules, then it all works the way it should. If we accept that we aren't the narcissistic center of the universe and that not everything revolves around our needs, wants, and desires we can start to look out for other people.

If everyone looks out for everyone, we're all looked out for. It's not all about me, and sometimes I lose. Sometimes I don't make the light. Sometimes I have to wait. If I don't leave the house early enough, sometimes... I am late. But I eat my losses. I roll with the punches. If I miss a turn or an exit, I don't slam on the brakes, cut three lanes of traffic and hold up an entire block of cars because I made a mistake and missed my street. I'll go as long as it takes to find a place to turn around and come back. That's just who I am. I'm awesome.

So, what spawned my story? Well, as I sat in the half-mile long line of cars, waiting to get into school I noticed something disturbing. People were cutting. I know! The nerve!

Seriously…who does that? I factor in "line time" into my morning routine. I only live eight miles from work but I leave an extra fifteen minutes open to go the last half to three quarters of a mile. I do. I get up extra early. I eat my losses. I just do it. There is no avoiding the bottleneck of procrastination and poor-planners. 3000 students, about 130 teachers, and a good number of other staff members all try to cram ten pounds of sand into a five-pound bag. It gets crowded.

But instead of waiting their turn, some people drive right down to the street and then jam their car into the line. It drives me nuts. I know it shouldn't, but it does. Trust me…I've been praying about it. And, I might add the Lord has granted me a certain amount of peace about the whole issue. Admittedly, I still root for the person who is being cut in front of, to pull up and refuse entry to the interloper. But, when it's all said and done we're all trying to get the same place. Right? School. If the students weren't cutting in line, they wouldn't be going at all.

Anyhow…here's what popped into my head. Keep in mind that it's not rooted in sound biblical theology. It's just a story about God.

The light was beautiful.

It was incredible. He hadn't known that it was possible to feel this way, even less-so how to describe it. It was like every molecule in his body were simultaneously being hugged by a warm, loving cloud. A voice spoke his name. He had never heard it before but in a way that he couldn't explain, he'd heard it all of his life. Familiar sensations of tactile awareness and temperature washed over him as he floated. Upward, he couldn't explain why but he knew he was floating up.

Suddenly there was a firmness underneath him. His feet touched solid, but soft, ground. The mist around him cleared in a swirling wisp and he found himself standing at the end of a very long line.

For as far as he could see ahead of him there were people, patiently standing in line for something. Some sat, others stood, while others took naps on the outcropping puffs of clouds that happened by now and then. Light drew his attention skyward and his mouth dropped. Above them were countless galaxies of every size, shape and, color. They looked close enough to touch. The clusters of stars spun and pinwheeled above them all in a choreographed dance of eternity. Nebulas changed shapes as worlds were created and galaxies burned out. He was simply lost in it. He could stare at this forever.

"Pretty great, huh?" He started and flinched at the gravel packed voice from in front of him.

"Whoa, sorry you startled me." He replied.

The man laughed, "Not to worry. Names Jonah. Not the fish guy, now. I get that question a lot up here." He stuck out his hand and waited.

After a few moments his brain booted back up and he hurriedly replied, "Tom. I'm Tom. Nice to meet you." Tom grasped Jonah's hand and they shook.

"What'd'ya think of your new digs?" Jonah asked with a chuckle.

"Digs?" Tom questioned. Jonah took a step back and made a grand sweeping gesture drawing attention to the white knee-length tunic he had on. Then he nodded toward Tom and waited for recognition. Tom's eyes widened as he surveyed himself, then looked up the line at all his new neighbors, then back at Jonah. "We're all wearing, this?" he asked.

"Yes sir. Looks like Heaven gets a bulk discount at the cosmic Walmart." Jonah said with a shrug.

Tom let that sink in for a moment, "Heaven. This, is heaven"

Jonah looked around and smirked, "Well it sure ain't Missouri. I should know. Spent 57 years there before I…" Jonah dropped his head to the side, crossed his eyes, stuck out his tongue, and gurgled.

"Died? You died. We died. I died." Jonah patiently waited for Tom to catch up. Tom finished connecting the dots, "Oh my gosh, I died and this is heaven, aaaaand, I'm going to meet God!"

"Bingo." Jonah replied with two finger pistols.

"When?! Where?!" Tom bounced on his toes and tried to look up the line.

"Pump the brakes there, son. You haven't even had your introduction by the welcome wagon." Jonah said as he put a hand on Tom's shoulder.

"Welcome wagon?" Tom asked. Jonah raised his eyebrows and smiled with a nod, telling Tom to look behind him. Tom slowly turned and was eye level to a red sash. A red sash tied around a massive waist. A massive waist belonging to a creature who towered over Tom like a parent does a toddler. Tom had seen drawings, pictures, movies, but nothing could have prepared him for this. It was an angel.

Dazzling white wings half wrapped around the being at the shoulders. It was an actual angel and it was smiling at him. Tom was speechless. Jonah smiled and extended a fist toward the holy messenger. The angel smiled and bumped the tiny knuckles back with its sledgehammer of a hand.

"Thomas Carlson Mathers," the angel asked.

"Yes. I'm Tom," Tom answered back.

"Thomas, you have been a faithful servant to The Lord Jesus Christ. You have lived by His word and followed His teachings. You have loved Him with your whole heart and He has called you home."

"Thank you." Tom didn't know what else to say.

The angel relaxed a bit, "What do you think so far?"

Tom looked around in wonder, "It's incredible. I never knew heaven could look like this."

The angel shook its massive head, "Oh no my child, this is not the eternal kingdom. That has yet to be revealed to you. The preparations are still underway. At that time which only The Lord knows, the heavens will open, and Jesus will return to retrieve all of those who follow Him who were left behind on the Earth. Then we shall all ride with The Lord in the air and defeat the Evil One before The Christ establishes His eternal kingdom."

Tom stared back, slack-jawed, "Let me help," Jonah interjected, "It took me a minute to get it when I got here, cause shiny face over there was talking in the King's-James Old-English and I didn't understand it either. This here is like the lobby of heaven. Sparkles over there," the angel's face dropped a bit, "is like the concierge. Our Lord Jesus is getting everything ready down on Earth and up here for the grand opening. It's just going to take a little time. So, we'll wait here." He looked over Tom's shoulder and up at the angel with a wink, "How'd I do?"

The angel's face was stern for a moment then softened, "I do not sparkle. I shine with The Lord's glory. But yes, that sums up your situation."

Tom nodded, "So, I have to wait to meet Jesus? Okay, how long have you been here?"

Jonah shrugged, "I don't really know. Time's kinda funny up here. But that don't matter. We get to be with Jesus. Forever.

Tom nodded in agreement, "That's all that matters to me."

"Excellent," the angel exclaimed, "Pray and rejoice, the day of The Lord draws near!" With that the angel vanished.

Tom, still mesmerized, looked at where the messenger had been for a few moments, then back to Jonah.

"This is incredible. Praise God." He said.

"Amen, brother," Jonah replied. Tom smiled and looked up at the wonder the Lord had made for them and began to pray.

———————

Tom prayed for time and time again. The line of people had grown beyond where he could see behind him. He had heard the angel give the welcome speech to each new arrival within earshot. Each time he smiled. Time floated by without knowledge. The Lord's presence was almost tangible. Tom was in the middle of a prayer when he heard a murmur running through the line toward him. People were talking. Something was happening.

Tom popped his head out of line and looked up toward the front. An impossibly long cue of linen clad people stretched off into infinity. Then a faint whisper began emanating from somewhere up at the beginning. It rolled and boiled in intensity growing as it grew closer to where Tom and Jonah were. It was a round of the Telephone Game but on a heavenly scale. The message got to the person in front of

Jonah, then to Tom. It was almost time. Things were picking up pace down there.

"The Tribulation started. We got seven years down there before we ride back with Jesus! Let's Go!" Jonah cheered.

It was then he heard it. From somewhere far up ahead of him came a cheer. It exploded into the air like a supernova and washed over them. Wave after wave of unbridled joy. The noise from any football stadium or rock concert he had ever been in back on Earth was a sad, pale comparison. It sounded like millions of voices calling out in glee.

Tom stood on his tip-toes to see if he could get a better look. The cheers welled again and shook the heavens. It was like a tidal wave of pure emotion. He knew it should have hurt his ears. His eardrums should've ruptured and been dripping down onto his shoulders like honey out of a broken comb, but they weren't. It just passed through him. It felt amazing, and he couldn't fight the urge to join in. A cry escaped his lips surprising him.

"Why are we cheering?" Tom asked Jonah during a lull.

"It's not just us, it's the angels as well, look," Jonah pointed up to what looked like a mountain made of clouds to their left and lining a ridge were thousands upon thousands of mighty angels, swords raised into the air in triumph, shaking the heavens with their cheers. "They're cheering on Jesus in the battle for the last souls. Listen to them, every time He wins someone away from Satan." Right then another roar ripped through the air and Tom raised his fists above his head and cried out.

It was then, arms raised in holy support that Tom noticed something odd. Each new soul that appeared wasn't going where they were supposed to go. When they materialized out of the mist they simply walked into the line. They were supposed to start at the back. Like Tom did, and how every other person who'd arrived since had. There was an order to this. This wasn't right. Or fair.

The people who waited, and waited, and waited to accept Jesus in the 11th hour got special treatment? They were cutting in line! He had been faithful nearly his entire life. Suffered for his faith. Gone without, fought temptation, and now his reward was being pushed to the back of the line by these last-minute converts. Did Jonah see this? He leaned in and shot a hot-breathed whisper into his right ear, "Jonah, are you seeing this?"

"Yeah buddy!" Came Jonah's joy-filled reply, "Ain't it awesome?"

"Awesome?" Tom asked in disbelief. "They're cutting the line. We've been here for, who knows how long and we did what we supposed to do. We waited. We prayed. Why do they get special treatment?"

Jonah put a hand on Tom's shoulder, "Tom, we're all here for the same reason. We're on the same team, amigo. One in Christ. Just be glad they're here at all. Jesus is winning our brothers and sisters away from a life separated from Him."

"I know... I know... but, they shouldn't be able to just cut the line." Tom sulked back away from Jonah who raised his arms up and let another cheer. He was not happy about this. They weren't better than him. The cheering went on and on and on. A few times he had to take a step back to accommodate the new arrivals in front of him. He began to pace. With arms folded and a stern pout etched across his face Tom stepped out of line. He couldn't take it anymore. "Excuse me. Excuse me. I'd like to speak to somebody please." He drew confused looks from the people around him but he didn't care. Tom was going to get justice. "I'd like something done about the people cutting in line please. I deserve to be up there, not them."

There was a flash and the angel of God who had greeted him was before Tom. "What is the problem fellow servant of Jesus?" the angel asked.

Tom repeated himself, "I'd just like something done about the people cutting in line please. I deserve to be up there, not them."

"You deserve to… hmm." The angel took a step back, considered Tom for a moment, nodded, then vanished.

Tom looked around trying to catch the eye of someone near him for validation, aggravated that he had just been ignored. Just when he was about to start making demands again the world erupted in light. He fell backward into a cloud and held a hand up to shield his eyes. The air shook with power. It was like warm water that soaked into his skin and wet his bones. It felt wonderful and terrifying at the same time. Tom tried to regain his balance but he couldn't. He felt so small next to the light. Then a voice spoke. Not with words that he could hear with his ears, but with love fed directly into his spirit.

"What troubles you my child?"

Tom gasped, "Lord? Jesus… is it you?" He immediately knew the answer to his own question.

"Of course, Thomas. I felt your pain and I wanted to give you peace." The Lord replied.

Tom was dumbfounded. The Author of Life was talking… to him. The creator of the universe took time out of the cosmic battle for everything to tend to little old, him. His mind short-circuited, rational thought had left the building, and he blurted out the first thought he could grab ahold of, "They're cutting in line!" If he could have reached out and grabbed the words and shoved them back into his stupid mouth he would have. The regret was instant. Shame and condemnation washed over him like sewage. Tom was marinating in it.

There was a soft silence that made a single moment feel eternal. He didn't know how else to explain it. It felt like the light of the creator was smiling at him. It was an amused smile. He didn't know how he knew that, but he did. Tom could feel the love pouring over him, washing him clean.

"*Who?*" asked the light.

Tom took a deep breath and steadied himself, "The new people. Every time one of them appears they just hop into the line wherever they please.

"*Thomas, why are you here?*"

Tom swallowed hard, "Because I love you, Lord."

"*Do you think that your feelings of love and joy for me are comparable to what I feel for you my good and faithful servant?*" He asked.

"I don't know if that's possible, Lord." Tom answered.

"So then why not simply rejoice when one of your brothers or sisters come home and are wrested from the Evil One?" He asked.

Tom's head dropped in shame, "I, just…I don't know."

Whoever welcomes one of these little children in my name welcomes me; and whoever welcomes me does not welcome me but the one who sent me. You are here for love. My love. You are all one in Me. Rejoice in salvation. Yours and that of your brethren. But many who are first will be last, and many who are last will be first.

"I am so sorry Lord." Tom said as he dropped to his knees and closed his eyes.

"Rejoice and pray, the time is near."

Tom opened his eyes and The Light was gone. He heard another roar of joy rip through the heavens and he joined in the celebration as he got to his feet. It was electric. He cleared his head and let the anticipation of another saved soul run up his spine. They were all going to the same place for the same reason. Just then, a wide-eyed young man appeared to his left. Tom reached out, put an arm around his shoulders, and helped him into line in front of himself. "Welcome home," Tom said with a smile as another cheer of victory shook eternity.

———————

As an aside, I am very wary about writing things that seem to put words into the Lord's mouth. I took some liberty in voicing things that I feel the Lord speaking to my heart and put them to paper. When I wrote the Lord speaking to Tom, I did my best to keep everything based in His scriptural teachings when I couldn't directly quote Him from the Bible. I hope you enjoyed the story.

CHAPTER SIX

GETTING WHAT YOU DESERVE

Ephesians 1:7

In him we have redemption through his blood, the forgiveness
of sins, in accordance with the riches of God's grace

One of the most commonly used phrases in the
childhood vocabulary is, "*That's not fair*!" Children seem to have
a very defined, concise definition of what exactly constitutes
"fairness" in relation to their small universe. Usually it has
something to do with getting a privilege, or some type of
sugary sustenance that is currently in the possession of
somebody else. Now this concept of fairness is understandably
skewed to the positive side of the spectrum. The older I get,
the fuzzier the early years become. But for the life of me, I

can't recall a single time that I complained about not getting caught when I did something wrong. I never cried and pouted when my little brother got blamed for something bad that I did.

I can't remember ever looking over at my brother's piece of cake and saying to Mom, "He didn't get enough, you gave me too much. That's not fair!" Nor in all the time that I've been around children have I heard a single protest when prosperity in the form of toys, or food, or an extended bed time has been graciously granted by a parent.

This construct that we develop as kids doesn't go away as we grow; it simply evolves and grows with us. In my profession I spend eight hours a day five days a week trying to corral, control, discipline, interact with, mentor, befriend and ultimately teach 400 thirteen to fifteen-year old's. To some, what I do for a living may seem like cruel and unusual punishment but I love it. The interesting thing is that the same knee jerk, he got more ice cream; mentality is there, they just hide it better. I decided one day to count how many times I heard the infamous phrase.

Over a two-day period, I was bombarded with the F-word (fair) over sixty-seven times. That means that in an 8-hour school day, my kids were complaining about something that lacked (in their eyes) fairness about 8.4 times per hour, that's about once every 7 ½ minutes. I must be a monster to be so unfair. But again, I don't think I heard a complaint when I gave them a night off from homework. After I made that proclamation it was smooth sailing. Smiles all around, I was the greatest. But you should have seen the tide change when I assigned an essay. The F-word was flying around like there was no tomorrow. Funny how that works.

But our concept of fairness stays with us as we grow. Driving down the 5 freeway after work I can't recall a time when I looked around, angry that an officer of the law hadn't pulled me over and cited me for speeding. Instead I silently weave my way through traffic, skittish and wary like a baby seal swimming in murky waters, waiting for an unseen shark to sink its jagged teeth into my tail and drag me away to traffic school.

In the business world you deserve the promotion. You worked hard for the raise. When you are passed up for the third time for making partner at the firm, the righteous indignation that you feel churning in your gut could level a small city. You are justified in your fury because you earned it. The reward, the glory, the recognition. Why can't they see how great you really are?

Why can't they all just give us what we deserve? Can't God see that I earned the (fill in the blank) _____? Well that's kind of a silly question. God sees everything. So, if He sees everything, why haven't I received my_____? If we take a step back and look at the big picture, I think the better question is do you really want to get what you deserve? If we look at our lives through God's eyes we begin to see our actions...all of our actions for what they really are and our fervor for fairness may begin to wane. What do we deserve?

Well, I can tell you what I deserve. I deserve recognition for the amazing job I do teaching the youth of America. I deserve more money. I deserve the rather large scratch in the side panel of my truck to be fixed for free because I didn't deserve that. I deserve all of the goodness, praise and privileges that go along with being a follower of the Lord. Now you look at me waiting for me to continue, eyes downcast.

I keep shifting my weight from leg to leg, a nervous twitch biting at the corner of my lip. Why? I think we both know. I haven't finished my list yet. I conveniently left out the other half. My shoulders slump in defeat; I also deserve to die...forever. I deserve to bathe in every ounce of God's wrath too. I sin…on purpose…with forethought, malice, and zeal. I deserve hell. Eternal separation from God. I deserve burning, searing lamentations of all of my awful deeds to be replayed for me in painful HD crystal clarity for all eternity. I deserve to get what I've asked for, more so than I deserve the previous positive reinforcements.

Do I really want to get what I deserve? The honest answer is no. Absolutely not. An emphatic NO! I thank God for being so patient and kind and loving, and that He chose to die to pay the penance for all of my sins. So, how am I supposed to feel when I don't get what I think I deserve? From a biblical viewpoint suffering makes you stronger, right? Should I feel blessed when things go wrong? What did the Apostle Paul have to say about it?

And we rejoice in the hope of the glory of God. Not only so, but we also rejoice in our sufferings, because we know that suffering produces perseverance; perseverance, character; and character, hope. (Romans: 5: 1-4)

Well, it seems the Apostle Paul thought so. But what kind of suffering is he talking about? I live in South Orange County, California. Religious persecution is thankfully not high on my list of fears. Surely what he's talking about must be the old-world style. Before civil rights, due process, and the

Geneva Convention. It must be getting fed to hungry lions for your faith in Jesus, right? It's talking about the people who were tarred, stuck to wooden poles, and set ablaze by Nero to light the streets of Rome for proclaiming the Kingdom of Christ.

How does that relate to me? No one is persecuting me for my faith. My life isn't in danger. How is my suffering bettering the cause for Jesus here on earth? How am I supposed to delight in a suffering that I just don't see as noble? When I have trouble paying my bills, or can't buy the newest iPhone that's exactly the same as the last three I've had; I am supposed to rejoice? When my kids are acting out of their minds, or I hit the fifteenth red-light in a row on my way to a meeting I'm already late for?

It can be remarkably hard to find the silver lining, at least it is for me. When things happen in my life that don't go according to my plan I have a difficult time celebrating the goodness of God's ineffable design.

I would LOVE to win Powerball. I think I would be really good at. I would be the best Powerball winner, ever. I tell God, "It wouldn't change me. I'll Tithe fifteen percent. I'll help those in need. I will use the money to do good, I-tell-yah." I tell God that I can handle the temptations. I pretend to have noble intentions when I but that Mega-Millions ticket at 7-11 with my morning coffee.

But to date, The Lord has been consistent with His answer. No. But why Lord? I want it. I deserve it. I work hard. I'll do good with it. Well, He must know something I don't because I've yet to hit the big one. Maybe He knows it would ruin me. Maybe He knows that money brings out the worst in people. That my relationships could suffer. My faith could get clouded by worldly materialism. That doesn't change the fact I still wish He'd give me chance to prove Him wrong.

The point of all this is I'm not too excited about what I deserve. I deserve burning lamentations of my soul for all eternity. I deserve pain and suffering for all the hurt I've caused, for the commandments I've broken, for my rebellion against God. I don't deserve a single good or joyous thing that I currently enjoy. If that's true then why I am not melting in a lake of fire instead of sitting here at a computer typing all of this out?

Grace. That's why. Jesus' grace. He measured out all of the punishment and monumental consequences to my sin. He calculated the penance that would have to have been paid to compensate for them all, and then He took my place in line. I heard Pastor Greg Laurie give an analogy once during a sermon where he equated God's grace to getting a speeding ticket. He said justice would be getting pulled over, listening to a lecture on the dangers of reckless driving, then humbly accepting your ticket. But grace… ahh grace – Grace would be if the ticketing officer gave you a speech on safety, reprimanded you for breaking the law, wrote your ticket out, but then before handing it to you he folded it and put it into his own pocket. He'd look at you and say, "I got his one. I'll pay it for you." Slack-jawed you say thank you and shake his hand. Not only does he pay your ticket, but the officer shows up in court for you, pleads your case, and serves eight torturous hours in traffic school in your stead as well.

That's grace. That's what Jesus did and does for us. All He asks is that we accept His love and follow Him. When we sin and fall short, He asks that we turn to Him for forgiveness and guidance.

Remember, the next time life doesn't follow the script you've written, and you don't get what you think you deserve, take a moment and remind yourself of what you truly have earned in God's eyes. Then rejoice that God doesn't think everything should be fair. We'd be in trouble if He did.

CHAPTER SEVEN

GET OUT OF THE BOAT

Matthew 14: 29

"Come," he said. Then Peter got down out of the boat, walked on the water and came toward Jesus.

―――――――――――

In the Bible, the Apostle Peter walked on water. Most people automatically connect that miraculous feat with Jesus Christ, but in the fourteenth chapter of Matthew, we read about how Jesus was out for a leisurely stroll on the Sea of Galilee, in a bit of a gale no less, and told Peter to walk out to him.

No big deal. We read that Peter got out of the boat and started to walk on water toward The Lord. But then poor Peter falters. He takes his eyes off of Jesus and begins focusing on the wind, and the waves, and the fact that he is, oh… I don't know, WALKING ON WATER! Fear and doubt overtake him and he begins to sink. He cries out to Jesus for help and The Lord reaches out and catches his hand. Poor Peter. He failed. He floundered. He almost fell flat.

They look at each other, Peter trying to catch his breath, blinking away the sea-spray, and Jesus patiently waiting for him to collect himself. With chaos all around them and a boat full of onlookers marveling in wonder from behind them, Jesus calmly leans in and says, "You of little faith, why did you doubt?"

What did Peter feel in that moment? Guilt? Shame? Relief he didn't drown? Maybe gratitude for being saved? What we do know for sure is that he had just proved his lack of faith in God. He fell. Jesus had to lift him up. How embarrassing. And in front of his friends too.

I remember for years as a young Christian, new to the faith, I read that and thought, "Boo, that's how *not* to follow God. I'd never do that. Great lesson. Thanks." Now that I am seasoned (sounds better than old) I see that passage in a different light. There's a message beneath the obvious one many take at face value and walk away with.

What does it mean to have faith? I guess that would be dependent on what you have faith in. For example, I had faith that the chair I'm sitting in would support my weight. I didn't even think about it. I just sat down. No debate or fear. I had faith. It's easy to have faith in things I can see. Things I can test. Things that can empirically prove to me over a protracted duration of trial and error that they won't let me down.

What about things I can't see? How about... air? I can't see it (that's not entirely true, high pressure system, Southern-California smog begs to differ). I can't hold it in my hand. I can't smell it (I refer back to my aside on smog). But I know it's there. I trust it will keep me alive, nourish my tissues, and I can feel it caress my skin when the Santa Ana's whip it out to sea. I believe in air.

Faith is typically defined as a complete trust or confidence in something or someone. Faith in love, humanity, in God. Faith in the hope that everything is going to work out. Faith in faith. Even atheists have faith. They have faith and believe that there is no God.

But I think that many people paint Old Peter with a very broad stroke. What we are missing is that faith can ebb and flow. Faith can be dented, or hidden, or momentarily overshadowed by tragedy or trauma. We can get lost and take our eyes off the prize.

Peter took his eyes off of God and started focusing on the storm around him. He let the chaos he found himself in get in the way of his faith in the Lord, who happened to be standing directly in front of him. He was human, and like all of us flawed, weak, and afraid.

Yes, Peter failed one test of faith, but what many miss is that moments prior he passed a test that I personally admire and hold in very high esteem.

He got out of the boat.

Peter got out of the boat. He did something that went against every rational impulse that a mortal, person governed by the laws of physics should have done.

He took his faith in God and put it into practical action, He had faith that God would support him on the water. He got out of the boat! That's crazy when you really think about it.

We just accept it all because it's in the Bible, but really take a minute and think about it. You're Peter. You've had a *really* long day. It was hot. Muggy. Dusty. You just received word that John the Baptist, the cousin of Our Lord, was beheaded by Herod. Throngs of people from across Judea flocked to Jesus for healing and blessing and prayer and encouragement. You did your best to facilitate some type of order.

Crowd control was a lost cause. You were pushed, stepped on, shoved, bumped, complained to, and possibly yelled at. People get grumpy when they're hungry. Later that evening you tell Jesus, "Hey Lord, it's getting late and we're kind of out in the middle of nowhere. We should probably send these people home to get a bite to eat and get some shuteye." The Lord shakes His head and says (I'm paraphrasing), "No, we'll feed them, bring me what we have." You look around at the thousands of people and then down at the measly five loaves of bread and two scrawny fish you've managed to scrounge up.

"Umm, Lord. I think we may have a problem." Jesus smiles a knowing smile and blesses the food, hands it to you and your companions and tells you to feed the crowd. The bread is never ending. It simply regenerates out of the basket as do the fish. You watch in amazement as a feast is seemingly created from nothing. Is there anything this guy can't do?

It's night. Jesus tells you and the other disciples to go ahead of him on the boat and he'll catch up. Catch up? Is he going to swim over? But you do as you're told. As soon as you cast off the beach a storm picks up. Wind gusts whip up seven-foot swells. Waves crash against the hull of your small fishing boat. Worry tugs at your heart. This is bad. Where is God when you need Him? Hours pass. Maybe you doze off, maybe not. Then someone sees a ghost. A cry goes out on the boat and everyone looks port. A hazy form looks to be approaching where you're floating. Cries of fear escape your lips.

Then from the water you hear a familiar voice, "Take courage! It is I. Don't be afraid." It can't be. Could it? Is that Jesus? Walking on the water? Am I hallucinating? Well, I have seen him do some pretty amazing things, you think to yourself. I have faith in him. I trust him. So, when he tells you to get out of the boat and defy every natural, rational survival impulse you have… you do it.

Sometimes God asks us to do things that don't make all that much sense to us at the time. Things that scare us. Things that push us out of our comfort zone. Things we could get ridiculed for, or looked down on for, or lose Earthly position or possessions for.

He asks us to do these things with no more than His word, and a promise that He is in control and has our best interests in mind.

Share the gospel with that stranger (What if they don't listen?). Share the gospel with your family (What if they reject me?). Give your money to the poor (What if I don't have enough left for me?). Volunteer, serve, and help (What if I don't have the time or don't get compensated?) Give that up

(But I like it.) Stop spending time with them (But I'll miss them.)

The point I'm trying to make is Peter deserves more credit for this story than he gets. God ultimately gets all the glory, but from a human standpoint wherein we can take a valuable lesson away from an event, I feel that taking that first step was courageous. Yes, he got overwhelmed by his circumstances; the fear of the moment, the chaos of life around him; the fear of failure or the lack of confidence in self. Yes, he sank. But don't we all? Who has walked with God and not fallen off the path? Who hasn't been overwhelmed with self-doubt, or guilt, or shame? How about lust, or anger; even hatred?

God calls us to step away from this world and into what He has planned for us. We will all falter. We will all fail. We will all constantly sin (unfortunately). Those facts are a given. What's most important is that we stay faithful and step out in faith toward what God has called us to do. The most significant step is the first one. And then the next, and the next, and so on. Sometimes you start to sink. Sometimes you slip under, but be encouraged that when you look up through the murky water you will see the hand of The Lord Jesus reaching below the surface to pull you back up.

So... Get out of the boat.

V. Nicholas Gerasimou

CHAPTER EIGHT

WHY WORRY?

Matthew 6: 28-34

Therefore do not worry about tomorrow, for tomorrow will worry
about itself. Each day has enough trouble of its own.

I worry. I actually tend to worry a lot. I say it's in my
nature. Now I don't know if it's a preexisting genetic
condition, a learned behavior, or a combination of both, but as
far back as I can remember I have been a worrier. If we take a
good hard look at my family history in terms of the chances of
a hereditary trait being genetically passed down to me through
my parents, I am pretty much out of luck. Both of my parents
have, and still do suffer from varying forms of panic / anxiety
disorders. But again, who's to say if it's nature or nurture?

I guess the question I want to ask is; why worry? Why

should I worry? What exactly is there to worry about? Nothing…except cancer, cavities, jobs, bills, love, family, children, forever, tomorrow, next week, my salvation, my doubt, my faith, my weight, my sanity, (my writing ability); I'm sure if I tried I could fill umpteen pages with an endless list of neurotic worrisome babble. Why? Well that *is* the question. Actually, "why?" is the question of our youth. It's one of the first questions we learn to ask. *Go to your room; WHY? Eat your vegetables; WHY? Grandma went to go live with Jesus; WHY?* Why is the sky blue? Why is water wet? Why does it hurt when I stick this in my eye? WHY?

We ask why because we don't know, or we don't understand. As a young child those two categories, *don't know* and *don't understand* pretty much encompass everything. The world is a mystery. All is new. All is fresh. We are learning how to be people. That all changes as we grow older. We learn. We mature. Many of the *why* questions get answered.

You go to your room because I told you to. You eat your vegetables because you need vitamins, minerals, and antioxidants. Grandma went to go live with Jesus because He called her home to heaven. As our view of the world widens so does our perception of time. We actually get *older*, go figure. We start to get a sense of our own mortality. We are going to die. Every last one of us. Nothing we can do can prevent that inevitable fact. Death is waiting. Gaining on us. Hunting us. Our time here on Earth is limited.

That is when the question changes. It's at that point when the shift from "Why" to "What If" occurs. We know our time is quickly counting down, so we start focusing on the things that directly affect our remaining seconds. What if I do this? What if I do that? What will happen? What will I do if… (you fill in the blank). I'm sure that to a certain extent we all worry about some things. It's kind of unavoidable. Part of life. But to obsess about it…ah, now that's a true art. Take it from the master. I am good. Now to tell you the truth, I really don't know why I worry. I think maybe it's that I'm a little too aware of the fact that I only get one shot at this whole "Earth" thing. The Lord has blessed me with one run through.

There is no practice. Life is the ultimate *on the job* training. I really don't want to screw it up. My problem is that I think too much. I overanalyze everything.

What if? I was once told by an old acquaintance that I was the King of "What if's". I may not be the King but I'm at least an Archduke.

Can I change things by worrying? Can I make them better? Better yet, can I make them worse? What am I doing by worrying? What does it say about me? Well, after much thought and prayer on the subject I'll tell you what it means. It means I'm selfish. That's right, selfish. Selfish and stubborn. Selfish, stubborn, and full of doubt. Selfish, stubborn, full of doubt, and, well…you get the point.

Again the question I comeback to is, "Is His grace enough?" Do I want His will done, or mine? Who is really in control? At least the answer to that question is simple…not me. It is painfully obvious that I'm not in control of much. Beyond my thoughts and actions I have about as much control over my life as a napkin has choice where to go in a tornado. If I did have final say, trust me…a few things would be very, very different.

But, I don't. And I am thankful for that. Think about it. If you had control of your life would you ever allow yourself to suffer or fail? No way! Well I sure wouldn't. Who wants to fail? I don't want to feel pain, but deep down I know I need it. More precisely, the Lord knows I need it. The Lord knows what I need to experience to become the person that He wants me to be. I wouldn't be writing this right now if I had it "my way". It's the whole be careful what you wish for warning. Who am I to think that I know what is "best" for me?

Does a child know what's best? When I was five years old I would have been lost in absolute adolescent bliss if I had been allowed to eat candy corn for every meal. That's right...I'm the one person on the planet who actually *likes* candy corn (little triangles of flavored wax, and yes I'm proud of it). I wanted to do it. I knew it was good. How could it have been wrong when it tasted so right? Fortunately for me my parents knew better. They knew that by forbidding me candy corn for *every* meal they were actually helping me. I hated the idea of eating vegetables but I wouldn't be the strapping young man I am today if they hadn't force fed them to me. Now my parents let me have the candy corn on certain occasions when they knew it was right. I was kept in the dark as to the "when" or "why" of those special times. Sure, I asked...and asked, and asked, and asked. But I only got the candy corn when it was in their will for me to have it, regardless of my want.

Think about it. Does that scenario sound familiar? Does that back and forth ring any bells? It does for me. *In his heart a man plans his course, but the Lord determines his steps* (Proverbs 16:9). Jesus knows our wants and needs before we ask. He knows why we ask for certain things even when we won't admit the true reasons to ourselves. Why do you want money? Why *do* you want power? Why do you want a girlfriend? Why do you want a wife? Why *do* you want candy corn (why would anyone for that matter)? My point being that if God just let us have all of the things we want right now, when we want them, we would ultimately fall. They would lead us away from Him. God knows who we need to be, and where we need to be in life to be able to handle the things we ask for.

I look at my life and my eating habits (which are quite good) and I thank my parents. By my suffering the wants and desires of the irresistible candied corn I learned what they wanted me to learn. I can now enjoy a small handful of the colored wax delicacy and be satisfied. Through time and what I saw as suffering I learned a number of valuable life lessons that I couldn't have otherwise obtained. It was all part of their plan. At five I would have eaten myself into type-two diabetes by age ten, at twenty-eight I know better. I still get to enjoy the candied corn I so desperately wanted, but now I know how to handle it. Suffering and want are relative to whom you ask. So I pose the question I asked at the beginning of the chapter; why worry? What are we really saying when we worry? Listen to Jesus' final thoughts on the subject:

> And why do you worry about clothes? See how the lilies of
> the field grow. They do not labor or spin. Yet I tell you that
> not even Solomon in all of his splendor was dressed
> like one of these. If that is how God clothes the grass of the
> field, which is here today and tomorrow is thrown into
> the fire, will he not much more clothe you, O you of little
> faith? So do not worry, saying, 'What shall we eat?' or 'What
> shall we drink?' or 'What shall we wear?' For the pagans

run after all these things, and your heavenly Father knows that you need them. But seek first his kingdom and his righteousness, and all these things will be given to you as well. Therefore do not worry about tomorrow, for tomorrow will worry about itself. Each day has enough trouble of its own. (Matthew 6: 28-34)

The Lord always comes through. He always fulfills His promises. The Lord knows what's best for me. He has a plan. There is a scheme. He knows. He wrote the script.

I have the ability to act any way I choose. I can trust Him and His direction and act by His guidance and teachings. Or, I can go my own way. I can tell Him that I know how to do this scene, and that my ideas on how to perform are much better than His. To this point I've found that the more I worry, the worse I feel. The worse I feel, the more I worry. It's only when I hand the reigns over to Jesus that I truly feel at ease.

I'll close with one of my favorite quotes on worry. It comes from Baz Luhrmann in The Sunscreen Song, "*Don't worry about the future, or worry, but know that worrying is as effective as trying to solve an algebra equation by chewing bubble gum.*" And trust me it doesn't work. I tried it a few times during high school; it probably helps explain why I had to retake algebra. So trust in the Lord. He's in control. Just deal with what the Lord gives you, one day at a time. He'll never give you more than you can handle today. Let tomorrow worry about itself.

CHAPTER NINE

THE WEIGHT OF SIN

1 Peter: 2:24

He himself bore our sins" in his body on the cross, so that we might die to sins and live for righteousness; "by his wounds you have been healed.

If I had to rank the emotions that I experience on a regular to semi-regular basis, I think I'd rate guilt a Hippo-in-the-100-meter-dash, laughable last-place.

Side-note: I was just informed that the Hippopotamus can in-fact run up to 19mph over short distances (sprints) and is one of the most dangerous animals in Africa; and that local lore postulates that Hippos kill more people each year than lions, elephants, leopards, buffaloes and rhinos combined. Ok.

I amend my previous analogy. Sloth. A sloth-in-the-100-meter-dash, laughable last place. That works. Regardless, it is a horrible feeling. You feel uncomfortable in your own skin. You internally berate yourself for being so bad, so weak, so selfish… so gross.

"What was I thinking?" you ask. "Why in the world did I do that?" you plead to the universe. Well, the universe is out of the office today. Leave a message.

So, there you are. You're left riddled with regret, and simmering in sin, maybe even cornered by condemnation because of what you've done, or said, or thought. But we all feel it. It hurts. We've all had a taste of the pain that guilt brings. Unfortunately, it's a part of the human condition. We sin. A lot; and at times it can feel like the proverbial weight of the world is on our frail human shoulders. I can personally attest to feeling what I can only describe as a pressure on my soul when I'm deep in the aftermath of the latest failure I committed (whatever it may be). A heaviness that kind of sits on my heart. It can literally feel hard to breathe sometimes.

I started to think about this at the gym. Why at the gym, you ask? I was doing pull-ups. With a bad left shoulder. It's a blast. So, I would jump up, grab the bar, do around six, then hang there for a few seconds to give my shoulder a moment's respite from the sharp-stabbing-knife-icepickblender-of-death-and-hurting-cornucopia-of-agony that lives at the head of my Humerus, and then struggle through the rest of my set of 10. It was during one of my gravity defying breaks that I noticed something. It was really hard to breathe. As I hung there, arms fully extended, tension holding my chest open and the weight of my body pulling down on the rest of me, it was difficult to draw in a full satisfying breath of fresh air.

From there, my mind light-speed / pin-balled from the Bajau people who live in the waters off the islands of the Philippines and Indonesia whom can hold their breath for up to five minutes (it's crazy, they're genetically designed to go without oxygen for long periods of time). Then to Guantanamo Bay and how waterboarding must feel, and then, because of the position I was in, arms outstretched, my mind flew to Jesus.

Jesus. My Lord, nailed to a long wooden beam, then affixed to another to form a cross.

I finished my set and dropped to the ground.

He hung there for hours. Weak, beaten, scourged, cut, stabbed, starving, dehydrated, sleep deprived. For hours he fought for every breath. But wasn't there more weighing him down? That thought gnawed at the back of my brain until later that night when I had to put this to keyboard to get it out of my head. We say that our Lord Jesus died for our sins, but what does that really mean? Well, let's do some math!

Let's look at the belief that sins weighs on us. How do you quantify that? If it had mass, how much would a sin weigh? Six ounces? A hundred Kilos? Five thousand pounds? Undoubtedly in this argument some sins would weigh more than others. Cursing at someone would weigh less than stabbing someone in the eye with a fork. Having an impure thought about a member of the opposite sex would carry less weight than having an affair and blowing up your marriage. Now that's not how God sees it, but for the sake of the equation we're creating, and our sanity, let's set the weight of a sin (regardless of severity) at an arbitrary pound. A single pound per sin. Sixteen ounces of sorrow every time you go against God's word.

The next criteria to compile would be total sins committed per person. To this point in your life how many times have you sinned? Be honest. If you can't nail down a number, don't feel bad. Neither can I. A BA-JILLION? (Which by-the-way the Merriam-Webster Dictionary defines as: "[a] huge, unspecified number: Used for emphasis") I checked.

I sin so many times a day I don't know that I could keep track for more than a few hours, or minutes… To be honest, my stupid brain offered up some colorful profanity which I just mumbled under my breath after I knocked my phone off the desk with my elbow. But we need a number for the sake of the equation we're creating, so let's set the number of sins per human lifetime at a comically absurd fixed rate of, five.

With our two set parameters: one-pound of "weight" per sin, and a fixed rate of five sins per human lifetime, we get a grand total of (drumroll please...) five pounds of sin per person. Five pounds; doesn't sound like a lot, and it's not. The actual sin and regret of a lifetime can prove unbearable for some. If we theorize about the actual number of times per lifetime a person may commit a sin, we are talking about hundreds-of-thousands, maybe millions of pounds per person. An unthinkable amount of burden for any one individual. Imagine turning off the light at night and snuggling into bed with the weight of three-hundred fully-loaded, four-door, Chevy Tahoe's balanced precariously on your chest. Sometimes it's a wonder that we get any sleep at all.

Back to what our Lord did for us. We have the weight of sin per lifetime, but Jesus didn't just take my sin, he took ALL sin. Ever. We have to address the question of people. According to the "2017 Revision of the United Nations Population Division, World Population Prospects", there are roughly 7.68 Billion human beings on planet Earth (give or take a few). That number increases by around 1.2% per year which equates to about Eighty-Eight million new passengers on this big blue floating rock we call home every twelve months.

If the reproductive rate of increase stays constant over the next 30 years, we can expect to be fighting for elbow room (and food, and water, and clean air) with just over 9.3 Billion (low variant) to 11.1 Billion (high variant) other people by 2050. There are many out there who speculate that we will never hit those numbers for a number of reasons. Some of these include war (nuclear and / or biological), famine, lack of clean drinking water, declining birth rates in developed countries (i.e. the United States) for social and economic reasons, and diseases like Malaria, E-bola, AIDS, H1N1-2-&3; maybe the host of once thought-to-be eradicated viruses that are making a comeback due to the anti-vaccine movement, a mass extinction event like a meteorite the size of Texas smashing into Canada, or a maybe yet unknown mutated global pandemic virus that will in the near future kill us all or kick off the real-life version of the Walking Dead[1].

Regardless, that's a lot of people. But that's today; how many people have there EVER been? Ever? Total? How many

---

[1] Written before Covid.

souls have played their part in the cosmic play before taking their final bow?

According to many researchers who've dedicated their studies to population demographics, one being Carl Haub, who was a senior demographer at the Population Reference Bureau (PRB), a U.S.-based nonprofit focused on global population, health, and environmental issues, the human species as we know it today began roughly 50,000 years ago. This secular theory begins with what is called the "Adam & Eve" starting point. Bearing no theological connection for the people it was named for, the theory states that around 50,000 years ago (many would like to, and have pushed that date further back) two mysterious people were the genesis of the human race we know today. There is no data to draw upon to prove the theory so a fixed number and date were set to facilitate the mathematical equation.

The theory holds to three bench marks. One being the genesis of two individuals, or the nameless "Adam and Eve"; Two being around the year 8000B.C. when we reached five million people; and lastly around the time Jesus Christ was born when humans numbered a little over 300,000,000. Using these three benchmark points, The U.S Census Bureau, The United Nations, and PRB puts the total number of people to have ever lived on Earth to be at around 109,947,781,641 (One

Hundred-Nine Billion, Nine Hundred-Forty-Seven Million, Seven Hundred-Eighty-One Thousand, Six Hundred-Forty-One, give or take a few) in the year 2017. Presently you would have to add another 2 years of population growth to that number to be accurate.

To explore the topic from a faith-based point of view (which was not as easy to find) I found some information on a Christian perspective of human population. The Institute of Creation Research, and Physicist and Bible Scholar Lambert Dolphin each had a take on the sum total of world population from creation.

In his paper "World Population since Creation" Dolphin speculates that from the time of Adam and Eve to the flood there could have been (at the low end of the spectrum); over 3 billion people living, to the high in upwards of 10's of billions. Some factors that allowed for these numbers to be plausible are named in the Bible. One was the lifespan of the average person. Pre-flood and for some time after the human lifespan was upwards of 800 years. It's postulated that the lack of pollutants in the air, water and food, and the atmosphere being richer in oxygen and better equipped to keep most, if not all ultraviolet radiation from reaching the surface were all major contributors. Adam lived for 930 years, and if you average the lifespans of the nine antediluvian patriarchs you get a lifetime of about 912 years. That's almost a millennium to live, marry and breed.

Post flood, Noah and his family numbered 8 and the life expectancy drops off dramatically to close to what it is today. After this time the numbers seem to stick roughly to the previous benchmarks set by the US Census Bureau. Dolphin puts the "world population at the time of Abraham at 5 million," and "the world population at the time of Christ, between 200 and 300 million" (Dolphin, 2007). By the best guesstimates, estimates, and calculations, all told the number of souls that the Lord has allowed to live on Earth totals around 140,000,000,000…give or take a few.

If we average the secular and Biblical totals we get 134,973,890,820. Let's call it 135,000,000,000 to clean it up.

Now we have the total number of people that have lived on Earth, the average number of sins a person commits per lifetime, and the arbitrary "weight" of a sin. But we need to address the heart of the matter. Let's push our calculations off to the side for a moment and look at what our Lord did for us.

The Lord of all creation chose to, of His own accord, by His own free will, under no other pretense than the fact that He unconditionally loved (loves) me…pay for my sins with His own human life. He chose to take on human form. Leave the wonders of heaven, set aside his Omnipotence, Omnipresence, and Omniscience to slump through the muddy drudgery of what is everyday life here on Earth.

He chose to be beaten, broken, humiliated, scourged until the pearl white of His bones shone through the holes in His back; struck until He was no longer recognizable as the man He once was. He was twisted, scorned, torn, and mutilated. He chose to be tortured. Mocked by his creations. Cursed. Spat on. Laughed at. He chose to be pushed past the point of physical exertion, where every muscle in His failing body screamed at Him to stop, He chose to walk up that hill. He let the men He created drive spikes through His wrists and through the long bones of His feet. He stayed on the cross. He didn't have to. He chose to. He wanted to. For a little over six hours Jesus drank in every vibrant, horrible tidbit of pain the human nervous system could process.

He could have ended it all with a thought. All He had to do was to wish for it to stop and it would have. In the garden He hinted at that fact. When the mob came to arrest Him, Jesus rebuked His followers when they raised swords and struck out to save Him by saying,

"Do you think I cannot call on my Father, and he will not at once put at my disposal more than twelve legions of angels?"
(Matthew26:53, NIV)

Our Lord wanted to go through that day. To willingly suffer...for me...for us. It is staggering when you think about the depth of His love. But now to my idea. The single thought that so unceremoniously interrupted my back workout. The fact that has led us through this rather lengthy (and I must apologize) and possibly boring, half math, half history lesson. There is a moment on the cross when our Lord looked up to heaven and cried out, "*Eloi, Eloi, lama sabachthani?*"—which means, "*My God, my God, why have you forsaken me?*" (Matthew 27:46-NIV) Jesus felt alone. Disconnected from God the father. In Habakkuk 1:13 it says:

"*Thou art of purer eyes than to behold evil, and canst not look on iniquity: wherefore lookest thou upon them that deal treacherously, and holdest thy tongue when the wicked devoureth the man that is more righteous than he?*" (KJV)

It was at that moment that many believe Jesus took on the sin of the world. God the father cannot look upon sin so at that moment when the inequities of the eons settled on our Lord's shoulders, God the father severed holy the connection of The Trinity, and The Son was pushed out into the cold. To put it in human terms we can understand, God The-Father turned His back. In essence he completed Jesus' punishment.

This is what struck me. This is what did, does and will always leave me slack jawed. Jesus took on the sins of the

99

world for all time. Just kind of rolls off the tongue doesn't it? The sins of the world. We say it without really understanding what that means. Now really think about that statement, the sins of the world. How about the sins of the last five minutes…in South Dakota? Still astronomical. The last two minutes? The last thirty seconds? How many atrocities occurred on Earth today? With roughly 7.68 billion people on Earth, how many sins, from envy to genocide were committed? (You might want to go back now to the meat of this chapter and review the material, were about to use it) How many in one day? A week? A year? Mind-blowing.

In that moment our Lord took on every sin from swearing to rape, from greed to molesting a child, from Mother Teresa to Jeffery Dahmer, from the beginning of time to the end. Millennia into the future. The sick feeling of guilt you feel when you lie, or steal, or hurt someone. The demons that must plague murderers, the sickness of the damned; It didn't fall on Jesus. It wasn't placed on Him; He reached out and took it. He fought for it. He placed it on His shoulders like a man puts on a coat. For us, He accepted responsibility for every sick, horrible, depraved, vengeful, hateful, lustful, violent, deliberate, sadistic, selfish thought, word and deed. For all time.

Let that sink in. The next time you sin (or are about to sin) think about that. Every sin you've done to this point,

Christ paid for, and every sin you will commit in the future is taken care of as well. Kind of puts things into perspective doesn't it?

There he hung. The weight of His body being willed toward the ground putting an unnatural amount of torque on His shoulders, almost assuredly dislocating them. The anatomical position gravity forced Jesus into made it impossible to breathe because the lungs were compressed, so our Lord had to push up on the nail that was lodged between the metatarsal bones in His feet, and pull down on the spikes in between the radius and ulna bones of His wrists to draw in air. Prolonged torture. Agony. Pain.

But there was more than gravity at work. What is the weight of sin? We came up with a ridiculously low 5lbs of sin per person. Let's do some math. At 5lbs of sin per person, with roughly 135,000,000,000 people having lived on earth so far that gives us a grand total of 675,000,000,000 (Six-Hundred-Seventy-Five Billion) lbs. of sin that Christ took upon Himself (leaving out the constant rate of population growth and new sins being committed every second that compound that number exponentially); it's still a cortex melting number.

That's the equivalent of 2,934,782 blue whales of sin resting on Jesus' shoulders. Now think about how sick you feel when you have to get something off of your chest. How heavy does it weigh on you? Can you feel it? Imagine…imagine what our Lord did for us. Imagine what He felt. The worst part is I am responsible for it. Well, at least some of it. But there are days when I feel like I'm there, at Calvary, deliberately pushing down on His shoulders while He struggles for breath on the cross.

What is the weight of sin? All I know is that it's more than I can bear by myself. I struggle fighting gravity to wrestle away a pullup. Sin pulling down on my soul is a whole other story. That's why I am so eternally grateful that we have a God that is so loving, long-suffering, and forgiving. Otherwise I fear I'd be crushed under the weight. I'm glad the Lord has broad shoulders.

CHAPTER TEN

THE GREATEST TRICK THE DEVIL EVER PULLED

"Quakerism Examined" by John Wilkinson: 1836

One of the artifices of Satan is, to induce men to believe that he does not exist: another, perhaps equally fatal, is to make them fancy that he is obliged to stand quietly by, and not to meddle with them, if they get into true silence.

The Bible says that at some point in time, there was a civil war in heaven. Brothers; created in harmony to worship God-The-Almighty, turned on each other and a cosmic fratricidal saga ensued. This pivotal struggle which set the stage for, well… us, was waged between two factions of an eternal race of spiritual beings that The Lord God created before He breathed life into His ultimate creation… humans. We call them angels. These angelic beings were divided by a voluntary violation of a loyalty ideology which was (I would have assumed) universally accepted in Heaven and intended to weave them together, but sadly ended up ultimately tearing them apart.

What was it, you ask? It was pretty simple. There is One God Almighty. Worship Him and give Him praise. He made you, and so on.

There was a particular angelic being for whom we have a number of names for. Lucifer, Satan, the Devil, the Great Dragon, the Crafty Serpent, the Deceiver, the Father of Lies, the Destroyer… the list goes on and on. What we do know based on scripture is that he was an angel of light. God created him to be one of the leaders of the angelic forces. He was powerful and beautiful; on par with Michael the general of God's armies. God elevated him to a lofty position in heaven and unfortunately it began to go to his head.

Then one day back in time immemorial, Lucifer made a proclamation. He declared that he was his own god. He bought into his own hype and demanded the same praise and worship that he was originally created to give to God. He was apparently also a gifted motivational speaker, much in the way Hitler was gifted at getting people to think what he wanted them to (I'm assuming Lucifer had something to do with that). He convinced one third of the angelic beings to adhere to his new personal life philosophy and doom themselves to damnation by rebelling against the One True God who created them.

So, they fought. How fierce the battle was, how long it raged, the actual violence or literal logistical combat that occurred we unfortunately aren't privy to. The Bible is silent on this epic event. What we do know is that Lucifer and his rebels were cast out of heaven and now roam the Earth. Again, the literal, day-to-day logistics of this existence is a mystery to us. But we are told that they are here.

We also know that God's holy angelic forces are among us, working on His behalf for the benefit of His kingdom. The word angel (depending on what language you're using: Hebrew / Greek / Aramaic) loosely translates to messenger. These holy beings have appeared to humans in physical form over the eons. We have a number of documented accounts in the Bible. They have delivered messages, given prophecy, and even supernaturally and physically saved people from harm or death.

This reality has always fascinated me. The fact that an unseen world is thriving in a plane of existence that we aren't able to see, but which we are at the same time intimately involved in. The fact that a legion of powerful spiritual beings that literally hate the fact that I exist are locked in combat with others who are dedicated to my protection and salvation through Jesus Christ captivates my imagination.

As I write this, could there be an angelic protector standing behind me, looking over my shoulder? Could there be another being, filled with hate and rage at the fact that God loves me and chose me over him, standing on the other side of my desk screaming blasphemies and lies at me that I perceive as doubt, or negative thoughts, or sinful desires? Does the evil voice flying out of that ancient mouth sound like my own in my head? Can they cause my anxiety? Throw me into depression? I'm confident my emotional issues are chemically driven, but is there a spiritual component as well? Do they fight over me? What does that look like? Do they have swords? Armor? I don't know but I'd sure love to.

Now, today in 2023, in the era of instant access to information from every corner of the planet in the palm of our hands, we have become a bit desensitized. As a culture we are inundated with dramatic images, horrific stories, and as Americans, reports of strife and war from the other side of the world. We are culturally numb to pain, and crime, and death. It's tragic.

But I have at times wondered why Satan, who is the general of the fallen army, hasn't made his grand appearance. I know the Bible foretells why. There is a time and place for him to do this in the last seven years before The Lord comes back. The script has been written. But I wonder why If Satan knows the end of the story and his ultimate fate, why he doesn't break role and try to change it up?

Defiance? Maybe. I think the more likely answer is pride. Stubbornness. He must be so defiant and filled with rage that he will fight to the end out of duty to his own narcissism. Anger can blind. Why doesn't he appear to us? Why doesn't he command his soldiers to take physical form and wreak havoc on the Earth?

The answer to that question has to be strategy. He is an expert on human nature. He has been studying us for eons. He knows our weaknesses. He knows our flaws. He knows how our brains work, literally. He is the father of lies.

If they appeared to us and made a public declaration that was then instantly broadcast on Facebook, Twitter, Instagram, Snapchat, TikTok, and YouTube, the globe would no longer question the validity of the Bible. Millions, if not Billions of people would instantly turn to Jesus out of fear and the reality of the spiritual realm. Satan wants to rule us, and ultimately destroy as many of us as he can in the time he has left on Earth.

As I said, he knows how the story ends. He has to know deep down that he loses in the end. He is condemned. An analogy involving a lack of peripheral vision and a swimming pool comes to mind when I ponder this truth.

When someone's hands suddenly meet you squarely in the back between the shoulder blades, and your center of gravity is violently propelled forward over the open expanse of blue chlorinated water, what is the first thing you do? You reach out and try to pull as many people as you can in with you as you go down. Misery loves company.

Satan wants to take as many people down with him as he can. He hates us. In the movie The Usual Suspects, Verbal Kint played masterfully by Kevin Spacey (current legal troubles aside) says, "The greatest trick the devil ever pulled was convincing the world that he doesn't exist." It's a masterful strategy. To let the sinful nature that resides in each of us to simply win out. Maybe with some subtle coaxing and subversive suggestions to do what he did. To be our own gods. To follow our own paths. To get what's owed us. To focus on the world and our sinful flesh, rather than on our God who loves us.

What can I say… it's worked pretty well so far? There's a quote in the 2014 film "*God's Not Dead*" that I think encapsulates this paradigm perfectly. In it a man named Mark is yelling at his live-in girlfriend's mother who suffers from Dementia and Alzheimer's. He says, *"You prayed and believed your whole life. Never done anything wrong. And here you are. You're the nicest person I know. I am the meanest. You have dementia. My life is perfect. Explain that to me!"* She sits silently in her comatose state. Then suddenly as if supernaturally her eyes clear and she turns to him and says, *"Sometimes the devil allows people to live a life free of trouble because he doesn't want them turning to God. Their sin is like a jail cell, except it is all nice and comfy and there doesn't seem to be any reason to leave. The door's wide open. Till one day, time runs out, and the cell door slams shut, and suddenly it's too late."*

Think about it. In a battle for the mind and soul that revolves around people choosing of their own free will to acknowledge and accept a truth about the One True God, and His Sacrifice for our sins through His son, the God-Incarnate person of Jesus Christ, how would you stop people from traveling down the path to salvation?

Would you manifest yourself in all of your horrible, terrifying, rage-filled, supernatural glory? No. That would polarize people. It would crystalize a binary truth and force a choice.

No, instead you would subtlety lead people astray. Satan is playing the long game.

You would influence people and play on their selfish desires. You would take eons to slowly chip away at the concept of absolute truth. If there is but one way to salvation and to God, you would introduce doctrines over the millennia that run contrary to that belief.

You would appear to groups of people across the globe and do what you do best... lie. You would sell the idea that there are an infinite number of paths to Heaven and to God. Chi. Shakra. Reincarnation. Nature worship.

You would set up entire religions based on worshipping legions of your minions who profess to be gods. Polytheism. You would set up your minions and lead them through thousands of years of foundational traditional religious establishment. Generations would be indoctrinated with your lies. You would become legend and lore.

You would appear to a man in a cave in 610.AD and tell him you are the Archangel Gabriel. You would then dictate a new holy book to him denying Jesus as Messiah. You would tell him that HE is God's final prophet. You'd give him "Pillars" to build this new offshoot faith on. Maybe you supernaturally give him the ability to spread his message to the world. Keep pulling people down into the pool.

Maybe you appear to a young, gullible, struggling man in Vermont in the early 1800's. Maybe you appear as an angel of light calling yourself Moroni and indoctrinate him with a new revelation of God that runs contrary to the simple truth of who Jesus Christ is and His sacrifice for our sins. You tell him that he is a saint of the latter days and to spread this new addition to the gospel. Maybe you give him a supernatural boost to help him spread the new message? More people down into the pool.

Look at every Semi-Christian or Bible-Based cult or group and you will find threads of commonality. The denial of Jesus Christ as God incarnate and a member of the Holy trinity. The denial of the authenticity of scripture and the need to add to it. The need to break the ties to Jesus's sacrifice as the only means of salvation.

Sound familiar? Maybe you slowly influence global society to fight against absolute truth, and accept an all-inclusive do what is right in your own eyes mentality. Slowly the lines between right and wrong, good and bad, moral and not, truth and lie are erased. The value of life, gender, sexuality, freedom, choice, expression all become fluid concepts.

All from behind the scenes. Brilliant strategy.

Splash. Splash. Splash. More people plunge into the pool.

If one speaks out against this Brave New way of thinking in this Brave New World, they are labeled Bigots. Hate-Mongers. Misogynists. Sexist. Intolerant. Archaic. Irrationally phobic of everything they disagree with. They are then singled out, attacked, defamed, and ostracized by the media and the masses. It's Brilliant. Then for fear of the same happening to them other like-minded people think twice about speaking up. They try to blend into the background or they withdraw from society.

Either way Satan has effectively silenced the people who follow Jesus.

Jesus said, "Blessed are those who are persecuted because of righteousness, for theirs is the kingdom of heaven. Blessed are you when people insult you, persecute you and falsely say all kinds of evil against you because of me. (KJV)" This is nothing new. Satan had begun to cultivate a culture of hostility here on Earth, toward Jesus over 2000 years ago. Nothing has changed. Will you be burned alive, eaten by lions, or stoned to death today for proclaiming the Good News?

Not in America. Not yet anyway. But around the globe Christians are persecuted socially, economically, and yes some are even murdered for their faith. Here in America some of us stay silent for fear of losing social status, friendships, jobs, (or do I dare say it) Instagram followers! The horror.

But be assured the fallen-one we call Satan and his network of fallen compatriots are all working behind the scenes orchestrating situations, both political and social that are hostile and opposed to the message of Jesus Christ.

So, in-closing remember, misery loves company. The fallen angel of light knows he doesn't have a chance to win the fight, so in essence he's going down swinging, or to revisit my original analogy he's grabbing as many people as he can by the back of the shirt and yanking them down into the frigid water of that murky backyard pool… in January.

Head on a swivel my friends. Don't be taken by surprise or lulled into complacency.

V. Nicholas Gerasimou

CHAPTER ELEVEN

$\mathscr{W}$HEN THE MACHINE BREAKS DOWN

Genesis 3:19

By the sweat of your brow you will eat your food until you return to the ground, since from it you were taken; for dust you are and to dust you will return.

The definition of perpetual motion is, *"[T]he motion of a theoretical mechanism that, without any losses due to friction or other forms of dissipation of energy, would continue to operate indefinitely at the same rate without any external energy being applied to it."* Wouldn't that be great? A truck that runs forever (he said longingly as he gazed off into the distance). Oh, if only. Or any machine for that matter. We want our money's worth. We want it to work faster, better, longer and cost less.

---

[2] Merriam Webster Dictionary

That same principle applies to us. We want to last forever. Our culture is obsessed with it. Watch television or doom-scroll social media for a couple of minutes and you'll be sure to see at least a few celebrities hocking anti-aging this, and vital restoration that. Outpatient surgeries to tuck tummies, lift buttocks, clear up aged skin, fill in the lines of time under your eyes, and help shift the sagging libido back into gear. Youth is promised at the bottom of every bottle and nearly all ailments can be fixed with a pill.

Getting old scares us. We fear the unknown. Death just seems so… permanent; and in a human sense… it is. But we know that eternal life with Christ awaits us after we pass over. Therein lays the struggle. Intellectually we know that Christ is coming back. We know that to be absent from the body is to be in Christ's presence. We've read the scriptures, we hear it on Sundays…we know. But keeping spiritually focused on God is not an easy task. We live in a temporal world, governed by emotions, needs, people, food, things, and day to day life. After a brilliant conversion or dedication to the Lord, the honeymoon period wears off and the sepia toned drudgery of life creeps back in along with the sin, doubts, and uncertainty that go along with it. As I've said before, God can feel very far away at times.

I've found that one of the quickest ways to bring God back into the forefront of my mind is for tragedy to strike. A cancer scare, a severe injury, a life-threatening situation; you pick it and I immediately turn to Christ. My father was in Vietnam, and he told me that he never met someone there who wasn't intimately acquainted with the Lord during a firefight. "Please God get me out of this and I swear that I'll _____ (fill in the blank)." They're called foxhole Christians. Admittedly I am just as guilty as the next of jumping into my own foxhole every now and then and calling on my savior (whom I've been ignoring) to save me.

As immortal as our culture likes to make us feel, there is an inevitable outcome racing toward us all. In the movie Fight Club, Edward Norton plays a man who is a recall coordinator for a major automobile company. He deals in cost, statistics, averages, probability and death. In one scene he is looking at the charred remains of a fatal crash caused by the faulty rear differential of a minivan his company produces, which resulted in the slow, painful burning death of an entire family. He gazes on the smoking black shell and flatly says, "*On a long enough timeline the survival rate for everyone drops to zero.*"

We have an expiration date. It may not be as obvious as the pink sell-by date printed on the carton of milk in the dairy freezer, but it's there. Stamped right on our foreheads; in ink that only God can see. A preordained date when we will no longer be good. A time when we will rot, stink, fall apart and be destined for the waste bin. We are not designed for eternity (not in these bodies anyway). This husk, bag of flesh, mortal coil as Shakespeare's brainchild Hamlet referred to it, or whatever you'd like to call it, is like a top that's winding down. Soon it will run out of juice and stop.

The Lord set up existence with a failsafe built in. The laws which govern our universe guarantee our demise. Take the laws of physics for example.

The first law of thermodynamics states that matter/energy cannot be created nor can it be destroyed. The quantity of matter/energy remains the same. It can change from solid to liquid to gas to plasma and back again, but the total amount of matter / energy in the universe remains constant. I guess when God makes something He makes it to last; not always in the same form mind you, but its here to stay.

The second law of thermodynamics is commonly known as the Law of Increased Entropy. This is the law that is most important to my point. It states that while quantity remains the same (First Law), the quality of matter/energy deteriorates gradually over time. It's the basic tendency of a system to break down. For things to fall apart. Hot coffee set out on a counter gets cold. Why? Where does the heat go? The fabric of your favorite pair of jeans wears out. Why? What happens to the molecules that make up the fibers which make up the material? Have you ever dropped a hand full of marbles on a tile floor? Why do they erratically and explosively disperse? Why don't they just bounce in place forever, staying uniform tidy and perfect. Why do they stop bouncing at all? Entropy. Entropy is why. The tendency of a system to deteriorate and slowdown. Energy disperses and things fall apart. The same principle applies to us. We don't last forever. As we get older this fact becomes more apparent, and more painful.

To give an illustration; I went for a run the other night. As I write this I am now 29 years old[3]. Not ancient by any means but not so young anymore either. In those 29 years I have done a lifetime of damage to my body, by way of a nine-year football career and the power-lifting that it took to succeed at it. I noticed that while I strode along the brisk evening streets, my step wasn't as full of spring as it once was. The outside of my right thigh has been numb for about 6 years now due to 3 herniated disks and vertebral degeneration in my lower back, but as of late it has begun to spread down my

---

[3] I am currently 45 and am laughing at 29-year-old me complaining about physical issues and chronic pain. If he only knew.

lower calf and into my foot. Stinging, burning, throbbing; ghost pains.

My body is falling apart and there is nothing I can do about it. Two doctors have told me as much. That is my everyday life. Now I don't tell you this as a ploy for sympathy. I tell you this because of what it brings to mind.

When I find myself in pain my mind automatically fires off in two distinct directions. This always happens, and it always happens in sequence. First my mind races to the past. I think of a time when I wasn't in pain. I think of how great and resilient a youthful body is. I begin to reminisce and long for a trip back to those days in which sitting didn't hurt, I could sleep an entire night through, and I hadn't had to think up the analogy of dipping my leg into a bucket of fire and needles to describe my state of being to an outside observer.

The second place my mind runs to is years into the future. I think of how bad it's going to get when I'm really old. I don't look forward to a wheelchair. A walker, fused disks, hip replacements…oh my! That worries me a bit. But the worry is by design; because when I start to worry about my future I immediately think of Christ. My real future. Eternity with Him. That centers me again and kind of puts my life back into perspective. I think that my pain is by design as well.

Sometimes God gives us pain to help us gain perspective…to keep us humble.

In 2 Corinthians12:6-7 Paul spoke of his own personal ailment,

> Even if I should choose to boast, I would not be a fool, because I would be speaking the truth. But I refrain, so no one will think more of me than is warranted by what I do or say. To keep me from becoming conceited because of these surpassingly great revelations, there was given me a thorn in my flesh, a messenger of Satan, to torment me.

Now in all that I've read, there is still debate on whether or not Paul's torment was physical or emotional. I like to believe that it was physical, if for no other reason than to feel that I can truly empathize with him. Maybe I need my pain to keep me honest. There is a possibility that it's there as a permanent, God inspired cattle-prod, to zap me back toward Jesus. Sometimes I think that without it I would have even less reason to turn to Him and pray. It is a constant reminder of where I'm heading, or to be more accurate, where my body's heading.

This type of eternal thought forces one to look beyond our, roundabout ballpark century that we get to spend on

Earth. In the book of Matthew, the Lord was speaking about focusing on Earthly possessions when He said,

> Do not store up for yourselves treasures on Earth, where moth and rust destroy, and where thieves break in and steal. But store up for yourselves treasures in heaven, where moth and rust do not destroy, and where thieves do not break in and steal. For where your treasure is, there your heart will be also. (Matthew 6:19-21)

Our bodies are included on that list. At the end of the day, one of the only possessions that we think is justifiably ours…is us. Our bodies. Hence the saying, "At least you have your health." As if to say that when all else fails your machine is still running; it will carry on. In the Old Testament when Satan was testing Job he said to God, "Skin for skin! A man will give all he has for his own life" (Job 2:4).

Sometimes I wonder. What would I give to have a new…well…spine? What would I give to be pain free? To be young again? To be honest, I don't know. I do know what I wouldn't give. I wouldn't trade a second of the time that my pain has afforded me with the Lord. The moments of quiet contemplation and prayer that my failing body has brought are priceless. I can't believe I'm about to say this but I'm grateful that the Lord has put a proverbial thorn in my flesh. It has given me a perspective that I would not have been able to gain otherwise.

So, what do we do when the machine breaks down? When the joints creak and the hinges start to catch and pop? When all of the molecules that hold us together start to go on separate vacations; what should we think? Panic? Run straight for the drug store, wallet in hand, ready to purchase youth? No, I think not. We should focus on the eternal. Know that a new perfect body awaits you with Christ. Imagine it. That single thought alone fills me with enough peace to push me past the worst torment. Eternal health. If I live to be 80 how bad can 55 more years of pain be compared to an eternity of perfection? I think I can manage.

Remember, when you notice that you've begun to wind down, break, rust, and falter; have faith. Jesus is the ultimate mechanic…you're in good hands.

CHAPTER TWELVE

*L*EARNING TO FLY (OR WHY WE DON'T)

Proverbs 14:12

There is a pathway that seems right to a man, but in the end it's a road to death.

I like the saying, "The road to hell is paved with good intentions." For some reason I've always found the imagery intriguing. A cobblestone thoroughfare that is constructed of not smooth, river washed stones, but lost dreams. What would that road look like? Little coiled balls of regret. A pebble of, *"church is too early in the morning."* Or the little harmless lies you told to get ahead; now calcified and black, crunching under your feet as you stroll. I'll bet it's a wide road. Lots of elbow room. It has to be. It has to accommodate a great deal of people. The Lord said,

> *Enter through the narrow gate. For wide is the gate and broad is the*
> *road that leads to destruction, and many enter through it. But small is*
> *the gate and narrow the road that leads to life, and only a few find it.*
> (Matthew 7: 13-14)

How do we find the narrow gate? How do we stay on the narrow path? What's the secret to diligence? I think that the better question is; why are we on the wide path to begin with? Are we blind? Do we really not see where we're headed? If I'm being honest with myself I'd say no. I can see exactly where I'm headed. I know what I'm doing and why I'm doing it. I just line my way with good intentions to make myself feel better about it.

Sometimes you may feel like you're out of control. Like you've stopped walking down the wide road and started running. Sprinting. Sometimes my life moves so fast I feel like I'm flying down it. When I sit back and truly think about it, the best allusion I've come up with *is* flying. I imagine I'm flying (not by myself but in a plane). Now realize that I am not a huge fan of flying. It just unnerves me. Sitting inside of a giant metal tube that has, at a minimum two jet engines, each the size of a VW Bug welded to the wings is crazy when you really sit down and think about it. I tend to lean toward the whole *if The Lord had intended us to fly we would have all been born with wings* camp.

To compound my uneasiness, I was watching the news this morning and saw that the AIRBUS A380 took its maiden flight. The A380 is the largest commercial aircraft to take to the skies in the history of mankind. Weighing just over 562 metric tons, (about 1,239,000 lbs for us Yanks) 73 meters long (just over 239 feet), 24.1 meters tall (almost 80 feet), and 7.14 meters wide (23.5 feet); the A380 is roughly the equivalent of taking a 26 story building, laying it on it's side, packing it with lead (and people…850 of them), and then asking it to defy gravity for prolonged periods of time, as it traverses oceans and continents all while scraping the stratosphere. It just doesn't seem right.

To this point in my life I have been in 7 (count them 7) car accidents (Only one of which was my fault) and I'm still here to write this. I haven't read too many reports of a plane careening to the ground from 30,000 feet and people just walking away from it with a few bruises and a headache. I like my odds on the ground, but when in Rome…

So flying it is.

Why…how are we on the wide road? Well, let's realize my worst nightmare together; shall we?

I often feel like I'm flying through my life. Like I'm in

control of my direction. Events, time, people buzz past at breakneck speed. Sometimes too quick to process or debate. I can almost absolve myself of blame due to the velocity at which life comes at me. Then something goes wrong. I hear a clank. A rip. Life takes an unexpected turn. A shudder bounces through the hull tensing my shoulders and clicking my teeth together. Then it happens. I hear the engines wind down. The whomp of the turbines slow from a maniac buzz, to a lazy thump…to silence. As I lose speed gravity reaches up and grabs hold of the nose, yanking it south. I've started to fly down toward destruction.

The plane seems uninterested at first, sauntering; listing to the left as we fall, almost as if it's thankful for the opportunity to slow down a bit and take in the scenery. I start to build speed. The wind goes from a whisper to a roar. My floating decent quickly transitions. With a violent thrust my intestines are pushed up against the bottom of my diaphragm as inertia and centrifugal force combine to thump the air from my lungs. I lose equilibrium and my sense of direction as the fluids in my inner ear slosh. I feel like my head is a mixer and a giant bartender is trying to shake the world's largest martini. I'm trapped. Doomed. My plane now ripping through clouds, straining to meet the Earth. I twirl and flounder; flip, dip and jive.

I know what's coming... I can see the shades of brown and green becoming clearer. Masses become separate and distinct. Tiny spider webs suddenly crawl out across the map, seconds later they're roads. Green pinpricks grow into trees. Adrenaline pours into my veins. Pupils dilated, muscles coiled steel, heart pounding like a piston in a Big Block Chevy; panic is sprinting through the corridors of my mind, kicking over trash-cans and breaking windows. The world spins on its axis and I'm upside down. Parcels of land look like a patchwork of misshapen quilting. Buildings, at first indistinguishable from one another, line up like solders at attention in rank and file, hugging the now clearly visible highways and byways.

Death is racing toward me. Air screams past the cockpit. The windshield vibrates. Metal groans with the stress of the unnatural forces being thrown against it. My bladder finally let's go and my jeans soak as my shoes pool with warmth. I am going to crash.

The speed at which I'm descending metal becomes very pliable. My plane will liquefy for a moment at the molecular level when I hit the deck. *I* will liquefy when I hit the deck. Bones, organs, skin, muscles, teeth and blood will, for a split second merge into one gelatinous mass wearing jeans and a tee-shirt before inertia, gravity, 4 tons of airplane and flames combine to erase me from existence. All of the possible scenarios rip through my mind as I plummet. How will it feel? Will I pass out before I hit? Time slows down as the stress hormones fill my brain. All of my senses are heightened. I can see, hear, feel, smell and remember everything with vivid, crystal clarity. I have a few seconds left. I am going to die.

The lazy mammoth scale of the world that has been slowly growing toward me now slams into high gear. Things that once rolled now fly. Details come into focus. Cars, colors, birds; a couple walking hand in hand in a nearby park. Terrified screams escape my lips. Not words, but the verbal expression of pure horror. More animal than human.

If only there was something I could do. Something I could have done to stop this. To save myself. That's when I realize…in my last moments everything becomes clear. As the hull begins to tear apart around me and the cracked asphalt first meets the nose…I see my hands. Knuckles clenched to white, forearms flexed and red, elbows locked. I have been pushing the stick toward my end the whole time.

It was me. I drove the plane to the ground. On purpose. Deep down I knew I was doing it. All I had to do was pull up. If only I would have just looked up. Kept my eyes on the prize, so to speak. It's the carpenter's creed, "You will hit what you look at. Look at your thumb, you will hit your thumb; look at the nail you will build something beautiful." If only I turned my eyes to God. If only I had left my old life and kept my eyes locked on Jesus; I would be flying now. Instead I locked on the world. I took my eyes off of the true direction and focused. It all comes to me too late. Too late to fix it. Too late to change. I am left with my final seconds; as the first supersonic shockwaves tremble through the fuselage and melt the steel and fiberglass into a flaming blob, I see clearly. It was me. It was my choice. It's my fault.

Why did I crash? Why do we fall? There are a myriad of other questions I could ask. Why *am* I backsliding? Why? I think the reason is that falling is easy. It takes no effort. Gravity does all of the work for us. Even a dead bird can fall out of a tree; it takes a live one to fly back up to the branch. We need to learn to fly. To actively follow Jesus. We need to keep our eyes firmly locked on Him. If we don't, we will all eventually find ourselves tearing out of control toward our demise. Plummeting to apathy, jogging downhill toward hell through the wide gate, as we stumble over the good intentions we tossed out to cover the rough spots.

Will I fly? The answer is inevitably yes. I have flown, I will fly again. I don't like it. I never will, but sometimes it's unavoidable. I know that statistically flying is safer than driving. Statistically I know. But you could compile all of the statistics ever recorded, categorize them, validate them, truck them out to my departing airport in a convoy and stack manila folders to the heavens in letters that spell, "*You WILL survive this flight!*" and I will still taste bile in the back of my throat when the engines rev. Adrenaline will still tell my heart that I'm being chased by a lion and that it should beat for all it's worth, and I will still hold my breath when the tires give the Earth their final kiss goodbye before we soar into the big blue.

The only thing that keeps me sane when I'm on one of those unnatural pieces of flying metal is my relationship with Christ. I know that if my plane does go down while I'm on it, my last moments won't be filled with terror and regret. I'll know it was my time. I'll know He's decided to call me home. I won't be "*weeping and gnashing my teeth*" as Jesus often described people who were left outside, or who chose to deny Him. Instead I pray that I will be calm, and at peace with Him (of course I'll also be praying that if it's in His will that He'd fix the plane).

So if you ever find yourself careening toward the ground; if you ever look around one day and see greed, lust, your new car, a beautiful girl, a website you shouldn't be looking at filling your view. If it seems like they're rushing at you and taking control; take your eyes off of the world, fix them on the Lord, and pull up on the stick.

CHAPTER THIRTEEN

THE LANGUAGE OF GOD

Romans 10:17

So faith comes from hearing, and hearing through the word of
Christ.

Have you ever heard God speak to you? Not in the
ethereal, spiritual sense but in the literal voice of God, "I can
hear you Lord," way. I mean if I held a decimeter up in the
room would it register sound? Would the needle dance at the
words of God? If you answered yes then I am eternally envious
of you. I can't tell you how many times I've sat alone praying
and waiting, waiting and praying. Eyes squinched shut, ears
straining, the silence ringing in my head; but all to no avail.
Unfortunately, I have never audibly listened to God speak.

Now this isn't to say that He has never imparted wisdom to me, or told me to take a right turn instead of a clear cut left onto a certain path on my walk; but it has always been in my mind. I have less *heard* Him as I have felt His will. I hear Him in my head, speaking in my voice, telling me what to do. At times it can be quite disconcerting because I can never quite tell if I am having a conversation with the Lord, or just talking to myself…which could be a problem.

Putting the fear of mental illness aside for a minute, I think to truly answer this question, and do the Lord justice we have to look at it from a much broader prospective. How *does* the Lord speak to us? Ask that question to ten different people and you'll get eleven different answers.

This whole topic came to mind because I was having a conversation with my brother last night while we were having dinner. He is a math person. By nature he likes numbers, equations, theorems, parallelograms and protractors. Right angles bring him joy and he finds beauty in geometric proofs. I am a health teacher who secretly wants to be an English teacher (That's a half truth; I actually want to be an author when I grow up…don't tell anyone). I like words. I get pleasure from expressive vocabulary. I derive joy from allusions, simile and metaphors.

If you look at our respective disciplines at arms length you might think that they're diametrically opposed. Good vs. evil (evil being math of course). As an aside, I retook Algebra 1 along with a semester of geometry due to less than stellar grades in high school if that helps you form an idea of what I feel about the subject that shall not be named…but that deals with numbers. You can see where conflicts might arise when two people who hold slightly different values are having a conversation about the nature of God and how He speaks to us.

So how *does* God speak to us? Well, our conversation volleyed for a while but in the end we rested on a kind of a begrudging consensus (the begrudging being almost exclusively on my part, which I'll explain). Our agreement forced us to choose "E" on the theoretical multiple choice test of existence, all of the above. God "IS"…right? He created everything. He invented everything. So by that reasoning He is the ultimate everything. Let me elaborate on what we came to.

My argument was founded on the premise that God is "*The*" author. He invented literature, poetry, prose and rhyme. He thought it up. He wrote the bestselling book in the summative history of mankind, the Bible. It isn't written in binary. The book of Psalms does not consist of row upon row of one's and zero's. It's God's *word*. That's how the majority of us are fed, by His word. The fact that it's His *words* we are being fed by implies some sort of literary device. I've never heard anyone say, "Lord, your number sustains me." The Lord didn't command Moses to write down the sacred equations on the stone tablets, instead He said, "*Write down these words, for in accordance with these words I have made a covenant with you and with Israel*" (Exodus 34-27). The Lord is the author of creation. He has been called the author of life (Acts 3:15), the author of our salvation (Hebrews 2:10), and the author and perfecter of our faith (Hebrews 12:2). Our Lord Jesus *is* The Word. "*In the beginning was the Word, and the Word was with God, and the Word was God. He was with God in the beginning*" (John 1:1-2). Words I say! Words!

And so my argument for the literary cause went. I thought I had a strangle hold on this one and my smugness must have been almost tangible. After my zinger from the Book of John I sat back and reveled in my victory. He was quiet for a few moments and then quietly said, "Where did *math* come from?" My face dropped a bit at his tone. It wasn't so much a question as it was a statement...a proclamation of war. "So...?" he said, cocking his head ever so slightly. Not enough to seem pretentious, but just enough to imply a position of power beyond his opponent's understanding.

It was at that moment that it all became clear. The trap

had been set, baited and watched. I had foolishly taken the proverbial cheese, stumbled blindly into an ambush. Dean's silence had not been due to being dumbfounded or in awe. He was simply feeding me enough rope, knowing I was going to hang myself. I had to answer--I had no choice, and I already knew the outcome. In an intellectual debate, you need not prove that you are correct to be victorious; you must only prove that your opponent is incorrect. If you expose the fatal flaw in their logic it renders their whole foundation unsound and useless. With that simple question he did just that.

"Well, God did," I answered, trying to sound as casual as possible, hoping he would let the topic die. He didn't. "If The Lord created math, who is to say that He doesn't speak to us through numbers?" He counted on his fingers as he spoke, "Math is perfect. Flawless. So is God. God is the *One* and only. The holy *Trinity*. On the third day He rose again," then his eyes lit up and he really got rolling. "Those are prime numbers. They can't be broken down, divided, or reduced. Neither can God. He is prime. Primary; The One. Can't you see the connection? The Bible is full of math." Then he stole a line from my argument, "He thought up math, therefore He is *The* mathematician. Who are we to judge?"

I blinked a lot, took few deep breaths and nodded. I felt like Holyfield after going three rounds with Tyson, my ears hurt. But at the end of it, he was right. Who am I to judge how The Lord communicates to us?

It got me thinking. If I equate life to a math problem there is no problem too big for The Lord to solve, no equation too long; He wrote them all. I remember a few years back when Dean was a math major at Cal State Fullerton. Every now and then I would curiously peer over his shoulder and watch as he slugged it out with his latest nemesis. Page upon page of foreign script peered back at me, taunting me.

There must be a center in my brain that shuts down at the very sight of algebraic equations. I can remember in high school when a homework problem went beyond a few lines to solve I would drift off, hear rushing water, birds singing, and come to sitting in front of the television holding the remote an hour and half later with Doritos dust on my shirt. It was all very surreal. I still don't fully understand the phenomenon.

Not Dean. He loved math…loves math. It all just seemed to make sense to him. He "got" it. Doesn't it seem that way in life too? That some people just get it? They just understand how to be a Christian. How to carry themselves, to walk, to act; they speak perfect Christianese. I find myself looking at these people with awe (and some resentment) for their seemingly effortless walk with Jesus. I look from them to myself and back again. How? Why? What am I missing? In my mind there is some vital piece of the equation that I have left out. I keep thinking that I missed a step somewhere, "back there."

I can remember when Dean would hit a dead end on one of his problems. He would frantically redo the current calculation. Over and over. Checking and rechecking. Then, when the wrong answer stubbornly refused to leave, his shoulders would slump in defeat and a sullen demeanor would wash over him. "It's back there," he would say flippantly motioning with his hand to the stack of pages where the dreaded mistake was hiding in numerical anonymity, nuzzled among hundreds upon hundreds of its equally confusing symbols and exponents.

The next half hour or so was spent rifling through page after page of handwritten madness. It never ceased to amaze me when, after my patience ran out and I retreated to my room, an exuberant proclamation of joy would bounce down the hall, thus signifying Dean's triumph. The problem had been identified, booked, processed, locked up and sentenced to a swift death by eraser.

Then the arduous process of rebuilding his masterpiece would resume. I guess I view my life in much the same way; it follows a set pattern. I go about my business. I try to keep a close relationship with Jesus. I ultimately fail. Why, you ask? Because I'm me I guess. Once I fall (after I get over the guilt), I look back at the past few hours, days, weeks…etc, to see what page the error was on. I tediously work my back through my life to a point where I can identify the moment, or the decision that lead me to this particular sin, much the way Dean worked back to find his mistakes. Is God in math? Absolutely. Will I ever devote myself to linear algebraic equations to glorify Him? Absolutely not. I do however recognize the beauty that is inherent in its complexity, and the great allusion that it makes to my life.

God speaks to us in every way imaginable. He is the premiere expert. He is *The* author. *The* mathematician, *The* astronomer, *The* botanist, and *The* scientist. I guess He speaks to us in the way that He knows will get our attention. Specifically. Some people hear God speak in the brilliant pastel tendrils of a sunset, others in the intricate mechanics that drive the nucleus of a cell. God can whisper to you in an autumn breeze or scream at you in the eye of a tornado. If you think about it, He is everywhere, and in everything. I was fortunate enough to be a member of a church that Pastor Skip Hietzig was leading at Oceans Hills in San Juan Capistrano, and he said, "The Lord speaks to us with the regularity in which He derails our plans." It may not be what we want to hear but, oh how true it is.

The last few bites of dinner were very quiet for a few moments after the closing arguments. The reason being; I was formulating the previous few pages in my mind as I worked through the points he made. I can be very stubborn at times. I have even been called bullheaded...impossible even. I don't enjoy admitting defeat, but I will when I'm bested...most of the time. As I reached out and took his hand I realized something else--God uses all things for His purposes. Victories, defeats...you name it.

God can speak to us in any way He sees fit. Mathematics, poetry, nature, love...or a healthy dose of humility and a good kick in the backside over grilled chicken breast and pasta.

V. Nicholas Gerasimou

CHAPTER FOURTEEN

YOU GOTTA HAVE FAITH-AH, FAITH-AH, FAITH-AH..

Romans 1:17

For in it the righteousness of God is revealed from faith for faith, as it is written, "The righteous shall live by faith."

There's a game that played at summer camps, motivational productivity conferences and sixth grade sleepovers. I'm willing to bet that at some point in all of your lives you've played it in some form. It's called the trust game. The rules are simple. You stand with your back to your partner, cross your arms over your chest, close your eyes, and rock backward on your heels sending your ridged frame plummeting toward the floor and a certain concussion. That is where your responsibility in this activity ends and your partner steps up to the plate. You need to have faith that they will reach out and catch you before your skull bounces off the pavement. That's it. Simple as that. You need to completely trust someone with your safety. If they don't catch you, you will fall…hard.

Important point to remember: be sure that your partner is physically capable of stopping your momentum before you begin. No matter how willing and trustworthy a hundred and ten pound man may be, two hundred and forty pounds…is two hundred and forty pounds, no matter how you slice it…or drop it for that matter. The poor guy doubled up like a folding chair and I had a bruise on the back of my head for a week. But the point is that he was there. I had faith that he would catch me and stop my fall. At least he broke it somewhat.

Faith is a funny thing. Many people treat it like it's tangible. A valuable thing to be possessed. Well, what do we do with valuables? We save them right? We tend to hoard them. Box them up. We act like squirrels packing away acorns of faith for the upcoming winter of our lives. I was teaching on Obsessive Compulsive Disorder in my health class a couple of weeks ago and there is a specific condition associated with the disorder called hoarding.

Hoarding can result from any number of anxiety disorders all related in some way to OCD. In it, the person affected compulsively saves astronomical amounts of mundane, everyday things. From toe-nail clippings to empty mayonnaise jars…you name it, they save it. There was a story of a woman in one of my texts that was given as an example. She hoarded newspapers. Years of them. Thousands upon thousands of bound dailies lined her halls from floor to ceiling. Closets, linen cabinets, every inch of free space that she had available was stacked with the news.

Walking through her living room must have been like jumping into the pages of a macabre version of a Dr. Seuss hall of records, where the dank pages of moldy texts pushed in on you as they clamored to finish first in a race for the roof. When asked why she kept the papers her reply was simple. Someone might want to read them one day. What if her granddaughter (who had not yet been born) wanted to know what the weather had been like on February 10, 2004 in Laguna Beach, CA? Well, she was going to make sure that she could. That was her rationale. That thought brought her comfort and eased her anxiety.

She felt that she needed to save these things. Had to. If she didn't, an unexplainable sense of terror washed over her. Fear of the unknown. What if I throw them away and then someone needs one? What then?

I think that sometimes we do the same thing with faith. We hold onto it for the "what ifs." I also think that at other times we misappropriate our allocations of faith. We believe in things everyday without even really thinking about it. I sat in this chair to begin writing, believing that it would support my weight. I didn't systematically test it with a pulley and lever system rigged with weights to see where the stress limits were, I just sat. We have faith that gravity will hold us firm to the Earth, water will come out of the tap when we push up on the handle, and our favorite television shows will be on at 8:30pm sharp because we believe that TV Guide wouldn't lie to us.

Benjamin Franklin believed in death and taxes, Peter Pan believed he could fly, and Mary Poppins was certain that a spoonful of sugar helped the medicine go down. I have faith in the fact that tomorrow morning the sun will crest the Santa Ana Mountains to the East and set in a brilliant flash in the Pacific Ocean just behind Catalina Island in the evening. Why? Because every day since August 21, 1978 until now, that's what has happened. I have just less than 10,800 days of experience that says the sun's going to make a repeat performance tomorrow. Like clockwork, to coin a phrase. No variation, no question about it. It's a safe bet.

It's when we come to the unknown that our grip on our faith becomes a bit tighter. We seem to be less willing to toss our trust around when it comes to situations where we could lose, or get hurt, or seem foolish. Faith in love. *Does he really love me? Is she cheating?* Faith in humanity. Or ultimately our faith in The Lord. *Is He really there? Is He listening to me? Does He really want me to do this? Why would He let this happen?*

Our faith in God seems the hardest to come by at times. At least it does for me. Out of all of the aforementioned things God can seem the least tangible. The hardest to reach out and touch. The hardest to see. If the phrase "*seeing is believing*" is true, then it's no wonder that it may be hard at times to put our trust in God. We have to believe that a God that we can't see with our eyes is going to lead us by the hand through the darkest times of our lives. That can be a bit disconcerting. How do we know?

As I pondered this, The Lord seemed fit to give me a great parallel, at a Starbucks no less. I was having coffee the other day, and I happened to see a man who had a beautiful Golden Labrador Retriever at his feet sitting a few tables away. The dog was so well behaved. It just sat there. Unmoving. It didn't make a sound. It didn't even really move its head much. It just followed everything with it's eyes as people passed. When the man was finished with his coffee, he sat up and said something I couldn't hear to the dog. It immediately jumped to attention. The harness that was strapped to the dog's chest had a handle that stood ridged about a foot from its back. There was a green piece of fabric on the side that identified it as a Seeing Eye Dog.

The man grabbed hold of the handle and the two took off toward the parking lot. Just like that, no questions asked, the man put his complete faith in a dog. He trusted it with his life. They came to a curb and the dog slowed, letting him feel the height difference. They stopped for a second as the dog scanned the lot and then led him to the sidewalk away from the busy traffic. This fascinated me. The fact that he could completely let go of his power…his control, and hand it over to a dog.

Well, I got intrigued and went home to do a little experiment. I originally intended to do a day in the life of sightless person, but it turned into about an hour broken into fifteen minute segments. I just couldn't handle it. Here is what I learned: I don't even trust myself. As crazy as it seems, I don't even believe in *my* ability to keep myself safe. Let me explain. I stood in my living room. Couches, coffee tables, chairs, entertainment unit, television, lamp. I know where they all are. I should…I put them there. I know how many steps it is from the kitchen to the couch, the coffee table to the doorjamb of my bedroom, and my bed to the counter of my bathroom. I know this because I counted beforehand.

Even with this knowledge, knowledge that I knew for certain, the second the lights went out…doubt crept in. Now I *knew* how far away the sharp edge of the coffee table was from the kitchen counter that I had my hand on. But when that blindfold slipped over my eyes, all sorts of self preservation alarms went off inside my head telling me to rethink my impending journey across the living room. Was it really six steps…or five? What if? With knowledge that I knew for sure, I still walked like a tentative old man, with shuffling baby steps and my arms waving out for support trying to fend off any potential shin cracking obstacles I knew shouldn't be there.

So much for my faith. What if? I made it to the couch and quickly lifted my blindfold just in case; half expecting to catch my loveseat impishly tip-toeing across the room to trade spots with a dining room chair. Everything was just as I left it. Six paces to the kitchen. Not five. Why was I so nervous? Where was the anxiety coming from? How in the world could that man grab hold of the harness and with complete trust and satisfaction in his decision, give his life and well being to a Golden Lab on busy street in the middle of the day, when I was having trouble crossing the cavernous divide of my tiny living room?

The answer is faith. He had faith in that dog. He had faith in the dog's trainers. And I have to believe that to be walking around a busy street, sightless, using a dog as your eyes; he must have had some faith in The Lord. The problem for me is that at times I feel that it would be easier to grab hold of that handle and let a strange dog lead me through traffic than give control to Jesus. At least I can reach down and pet the dog. We don't like to relinquish control, or at least I don't.

I like control. It makes me feel good. I think that we like to feel proactive in our lives. Look around a Southern California freeway at rush hour. If you could put the definition of futile proactive helplessness into tangible action it would have to be in the form of the aggravated impatient gridlocked motorist. Why do we change lanes in traffic?

Does it really get us to our destination any faster? After 14 years of experimentation I can answer with a vehement NO! It just gives me the illusion of control. Like I said before it just makes me feel good (In actuality it just seems to infuriate me to the point of blood vessel bursting rage when the lane I just cut off two people to get out of speeds up the *instant* I leave it and the blue minivan that was three cars behind me scoots past and putts off out of sight as I stew in my now frozen parking lot).

In our hearts we take control of our lives and we expect God to follow suit and stick to the path that we've laid out. We know what we want. We know how we want things to turn out. WE KNOW! When it doesn't happen exactly "that way" ("that way" being "our way") we get upset. The moment we let selfish anger and envy fill our heads, and more importantly, our hearts, we give Satan a foothold. Trust me, when he finds one he doesn't like to let go.

It's all about the whole destiny vs. coincidence argument. One of the biggest problems for us humans is that we can only see God's plan in hindsight. It's only when we stop, turn around, and look back that we see the path we've been following. The "what ifs" and "if only's" kind of fall away when you look back at the big picture of your past. The Lord has led you along to help make you who you are. The only way that you could be you is if you did exactly what you've done, up until this point in your life.

So the path behind us is lit by our experience. But when we turn back around and face the future we are faced with nothing but total darkness. That's scary. The unknown. We have no control. The wind rustles the bushes, and a dusty tumbleweed rolls by, and for a second you feel alone. That's when Satan attacks, when you feel vulnerable. He attacks with subtle suggestions, not with power. He's the one who tells us that we can do it alone. He's the one who whispers that we should blaze our own path through the darkness. Get what's ours. Show the world who's boss. God? Who needs God? I can do this by myself. I-am-powerful. But at those moments, what we often don't see is the truth standing right in front of our faces. While Satan is standing behind us, busy pouring lie after lie into our open ears, The Lord is right there waiting. Waiting for us to accept His love and trust Him. To have faith in him. Waiting for us to follow. The reason that we can't see the path in front of us is because we are walking behind The Lord. He blocks our view of what's coming. That's why we've got to have faith. Faith in Jesus that He knows where He's going.

Keep reminding yourself, "a walk, a walk, a walk" it's our walk with Jesus. So when you get to rough ground admit defeat. When you're looking up at the rocky hillside, don't get too full of yourself. When the lights go out and shadows of doubt are swirling around you don't try to walk around your living room by yourself, you may walk into the coffee table. It will hurt. Reach out for help.

Sometimes the *right* route from point A to point B isn't a straight line. Yes, it may be the shortest, but is it what God wants? Don't take the course *you* think is best. There's a good chance it's not the one God has in mind for you. You may end up falling and getting hurt. Or even more frightening is that God may actually grant you your wish and truly give you what you deserve. Don't risk it.

So, faith? What *is* faith? How do we get it? Where in the world does it come from? How do we trust? What made it so easy for that man to grab hold of that plastic bar and let a dog lead him through the trials of the Starbucks parking lot…let alone life? A better question is: how can we trust a God we can't see or touch to lead us when some of us don't even trust ourselves? That's a question only you can answer. You have to choose to let go. Choose to relinquish control and hand over the reigns of your life to Jesus. What's the worst that can happen? Your life goes on status quo? What if you let go and you fall?

Maybe that's what the Lord had in mind for you. Nobody ever said being a follower of Jesus would be easy, or painless, or result in a fun-filled prosperous life. Actually, it is spoken about time and again how difficult it is and will be to follow Christ. In his first letter to the scattered Christian church Peter said,

Dear friends, do not be surprised at the painful trial you are suffering, as though something strange were happening to you. But rejoice that you participate in the sufferings of Christ, so that you may be overjoyed when his glory is revealed (1 Peter 4: 12-13).

Trust in Him that He's leading you where you need to go, to become who He needs you to be. Cross your arms, close your eyes, and fall back. He'll catch you. Follow His lead. Trust Him. He knows the way. More precisely, He *is* the way. He'll get you there. Just have faith and follow Him. Reach out, take His hand, and let Him lead you through the rough times. *However, if you suffer as a Christian, do not be ashamed, but praise God that you bear that name (1 Peter 4:16)* Just remember…you gotta' have faith.

CHAPTER FIFTEEN

RUNNING WITH GOD

Hebrews 12:1

Let us run with perseverance the race marked out for us

I listened to a testimonial in church a few weeks ago. It was very similar to the vast majority of testimonials that I've heard before. Life was rough. Maybe there were some drugs, some drinking, too much sex and not enough praying. Maybe there was no God at all in their life to pray to. They didn't know Him or care to. They were just lost. Floundering around in the darkness looking for meaning where there was none.

There is always a breaking point. A moment when they hit bottom. Despair. Hopeless. Sometimes there are thoughts of suicide. The loved one leaves. Breaks their heart. I don't know, it's always something. But it's what happens next that always gives me pause.

I look like one of the RCA dogs listening to the record in those old Christmas commercials; head cocked to the side, a pensive confused expression betraying the somber revenant approval I'm supposed to have when listening to a heart-felt testimonial.

They always say, "I can remember it like it was yesterday." There it is. The "It". They say it like the moment was an act of nature. Like a tornado or an earthquake. And don't get me wrong, maybe it was for them and God bless them. But they always have a moment. A definitive event. "October 13, 2006. I was sitting on the floor of my apartment, I'd been crying for hours. There was an empty twelve pack crumpled next to me on my left, and a loaded nine millimeter to my right. I was done. Empty. I was at my wits end and anything was better than how I felt. I was going to end it. A bullet to the brainpan and splat, all the pain would end. I'm not sure why I waited. Maybe I was scared.

You know, a part of it is always a cry for help. It's like the Hollywood movie version of hope. Someone always comes in at just the right moment. They forgot their keys, or needed to borrow a cup of sugar and, "Oh my God! John! What are you doing?" Well, I got the help of all help, but it wasn't my neighbor. That's when I heard Him. I had my finger on the trigger; just a couple more pounds of pressure and my couch would have been turned into an impressionist artistic rendering of tie-dyed sorrow, and He called my name. It all just made sense. I threw the gun across the room, knelt right there, and gave my life to Jesus."

Boom. Just like that. They have their moment that they can talk about in church. And from then on their life is measured in relation to that miraculous moment. Its like B.C and A.D. Before and after. Now they build churches, and give to the poor, save babies, pray 12 hours a day, and are wonderful magical Christians who have their moment and their story and their wonderful new life.

I write this not because I don't believe them, nor because I don't love them, because I do. I write this because…well because I'm jealous. There I said it. You happy? I'm Jealous of them and their moment. I want one. I think it would be great to have a defining experience with God somewhere in my life. The catalyst that changed me forever. Made me a new creation in Christ. A time I can point to and say, "See, I used to be like that, say things like that, think like that, desire those things, do those things." Well, I don't.

As I thought about this and scowled away in God's house, an analogy popped into my head. Running. Running with God. Well, to be honest the *first* analogy that popped into my head was running *from* God. I guess that really seems more accurate.

I feel like I've been running from Him my whole life. The question is why? Why run? Why am I trying to escape? Escape from what? If you're a runner and have ever been trail running my mindset may make a bit more sense. Let me explain.

Trail running is great. You're outside, it's a warm summer day and a cool ocean breeze is sailing up through the Laguna Canyons putting a hint of salt on your tongue. You are alone. At peace. It's just you, nature and your thoughts. All you can hear is the wind rustling the leaves around you and your own footfalls rhythmically thudding the ground.

The trails are narrow. They wind up the canyon walls twisting with a schizophrenic sense of reason. Right, left, up down. Switchbacks and near vertical climbs with steps carved out of rock or pounded into existence by legions of semi masochists like yourself. There are moments of breathtaking beauty tempered by flashes of mind numbing pain. Running is balance. Pain for pleasure. The journey is the reward and a dozen other poignant catchphrases that tell you all about the grab-bag of intrinsic and extrinsic goodies that await those brave enough to test the mantra.

It's while you're on one of these trails that you feel it. A presence. A force. It's as if you can feel the air change around you. A pressure variant fluctuates and all of the sudden you're not alone anymore. You can't quite explain the sensation but you're sure you can almost feel someone pushing up on you. It's a very disconcerting feeling. Like being positive that you've latched the public bathroom stall door and once the seats been wiped, the safety butt gasket is down and the pants are around the ankles and you've let yourself relax, you come face to face with a wide eyed uninvited new roommate who is in so much shock they just lock eyes with you for two horrifying violating moments before they slam the door and hurriedly apologize in a fading mumble as they leave. You're just left with the aftermath, and the inability to unclench.

The moments on the trail I'm describing feel much the same to me. An invasion into my personal sanctuary. I imagine Superman would have felt much the same way if he was taking some much needed alone time up in the Fortress of Solitude and just as he slips off the old red leather boots and kicks back with an *ice cold* one (Get it? Ice cold? You see, its ice cold because the fortress is made of crystals in the middle of the

Arctic Cir…never mind) a group of shutter-bugging Japanese tourists come shuffling in and click away recording every square inch. Just wrong.

So I feel it. Feel them. Pacing me. Gaining on me. Now for some strange reason I don't want to let them know, that I know that they're there. I just keep running acting unaware. The feeling grows stronger and maybe I finally hear a twig snap or a heavy hitching breath from somewhere off behind me. I don't turn my head, no…never turn my head. I just pick up my own pace ever so slightly. Not enough to let on that I am doing anything out of the ordinary, but enough to create a little distance from my new drafter. I'm not sure why. Maybe it's a macho testosterone thing, maybe pride, maybe its like when I was a kid alone in my room at night and the monster would come creeping out the closet and slink across the span of carpet toward my bed.

If I pretended like I was asleep and didn't know it was there, it always seemed to get bored and leave. It was an unspoken mutual understanding that we both naturally slid into. But I was positive that if I gave the slightest inclination that I knew it was there, a whimper, a sudden movement, perish the thought of moving the blanket and making eye contact with that drooling maniac face hovering just above my cover cloaked head, it would have slid a pulsating scaled arm under the sheets and dragged me off to be the main ingredient in some demon stew. Point is if you ignore it, it would go away. Sadly a chunk of that undesirable coping mechanism has found its way into my adult bag of life skills and has become increasingly less effective the older I get.

So I keep running. Blocking the trail, keeping my pace, trying to slyly pull away and regain my bubble of sanctuary. The feeling of being watched is maddening. I can almost imagine them staring at my back. Judging me. Why am I so slow? Why won't I get out of their way? Are they mocking my running shoes? My clothes? Do I have mud on my socks? Have they noticed that my right foot turns in more than my left and clips my left calf every stride I take when I get tired? Have they? Who are they? What makes them think that they're so much better than I am? What right do they have? Why couldn't they have taken a different path? Why?

So what I'm left with is this: I'm on a path that I like. No, I love it. I feel good on it. I'm comfortable and I'm in control. All of the sudden I feel that I'm not alone. I can sense someone else there. I can't see them, can't really hear them or feel them but I know they're there. In my mind I imagine them judging me. Giving me the once over and picking me apart for all of my faults that they see. I know deep down that they're better than I am…they did catch up to me and are in position to pass. My annoyance turns to dislike and my dislike to anger. I'm angry with them for judging me. I'm angry with them for being better than I am. I'm angry at myself for lacking. I'm mad at myself for not being perfect and giving the judging jogger any ammunition at all. Also an important fact to remember is that up until this point it has been a very one-sided relationship.

I posed the questions earlier, why am I running from God? What am I running from? Why am I trying to escape? Maybe I feel like He's the judging jogger. Perfect. Unwavering in His awesomeness and in my analogy, cardiovascular running ability. I can't see Him. I can't touch Him. I can only sense He's there at times. I hear something stir in my spirit. I see His hand move in my life.

Automatically I turn. I run. I can feel His gaze fall over me. Imperfect me. Flawed. Broken. Full of sin, and greed, and lust and anger. Full of the desire not to stop being any of those things. So in my mind I have to run. Escape from Him. I get angry with Him for making me feel this way but in reality I'm mad at myself for being so weak. That only fuels my anger at Him. Fuels my desire to run.

I said at the beginning that I'm jealous of all of those people who have their magical definitive moment with God to hang their collective spiritual hats on. I said that I wanted one, yet I continue to run. What if that jogger behind me is there for a reason? What if one day I give up? What if I just stop and look over, turn my head? What if I relinquish my grip on my own pride and let it float away like a Mylar birthday balloon on a windy day? What if? What if I turn my head and say hello?

What if Jesus has been keeping pace for all of these years just waiting for me to let Him catch up? Waiting for me to slow down and share the path with Him? What if my definitive moment is looking over one day and seeing that my Lord and Savior Jesus Christ has been by my side all along just waiting for me to acknowledge Him? It kind of makes you think twice about being rude on the trail. Maybe from now on I'll make it a point to stop and say a quick hello to my trail mates. You never know who you're running with.

V. Nicholas Gerasimou

CHAPTER SIXTEEN

*H*AVE 2 AND 2 ALWAYS BEEN FOUR?

John 14:6

Jesus said to him, "I am the way, and the truth, and the life. No one comes to the Father except through me.

David Mitchell – Cloud Atlas

Truth is singular. It's versions are mistruths

I was listening to an argument on television last night. I was lounging on the couch mindlessly flipping through the channels, looking for something to pacify me while I wasted time. Now very rarely do I venture up into the uncharted territory of the independent cable access stations. There is some scary stuff there. Strange stuff. More precisely, strange people. Strange people with even stranger ideas. I could go on but you get the point. I digress.

You can find two people sitting across from each other in purple plastic chairs, in a poorly lit studio, hashing it out about almost anything on every other click of the button. Sometimes it's like the poor, poor man's Jerry Springer. Other times it can be quite entertaining. It was on one of these stations that I happened to stumble upon a religious debate, and I'm always up for a good slug-fest.

It was the heated response of one of the men that got my attention, and paused my thumb over the button. He was so vehement about making his point that he almost popped out of his seat. His counterpart was very calm and collected, almost amused at his opponent's fury. I pegged it as quiet confidence; others might have called him smug. They were going back and forth about paths to God, what the nature of spirituality was, and finally, the concept of absolute truth. Three potential powder kegs of theology. That sounded like it could at least be interesting for a while.

They volleyed for a bit. The man who stood for the belief in a sovereign, omnipotent, omnipresent, omniscient God who so loved the world and the humans He created in it, that he gave His one and only son as a sacrifice for the sins of those people, and that whoever believes in Him and follows Him, shall not perish in eternal death and separation from their creator, but have everlasting life… (Whew, deep breath) kept calmly stating his unflinching viewpoint. He quoted the Bible, stuck to his guns, and presented some pretty clever logic traps that his opponent more than gladly stumbled into on more than a few occasions.

The man for the belief that all roads lead to the ebbing eternal consciousness, and that we all have our own paths to walk before we can become connected to the communal spiritual oneness that inhabits all souls, and the all great she-god can be communed with by nature worship, mediation, and conversing with the spirit guides of the dead… (I'm winded from just writing that) seemed a bit more defensive and animated. He accused Christians of being bigoted, intolerant, hypocrites, who only find the faults in people and spew their biased, narrow-minded propaganda with an air of superiority that drive the masses away in droves. This was getting good.

The spiritualist leaned forward and fired off a solid shot that he seemed fairly pleased with. He counted on his fingers as he spoke, "What makes your idea the only idea? Why do you people always have to be right? Why can't you admit that we both can be right at the same time, and we can both reach the same place by taking different paths? Why? Why do you insist on shoving your bigoted theology down my throat without even considering my viewpoint before dismissing it as bleep? (Substitution mine. You gotta love cable access) He sat back, crossed his arms and smirked while he waited for a response.

The "Go-God" man (as I started to call him) sat silent for a second and then smiled and asked, "What do two and two equal when you add them up?"

"Captain Blood-Vessel" as I dubbed the red-faced spiritualist, (It was late and I was bored) blinked hard for a moment as if weighing the possibility of the question being a trap; it obviously wasn't the response he was expecting to his articulate battery of poignant quandaries. He shrugged and answered, "Four. I don't see what that has to do with my question. Is that all you have?"

Go-God smirked and said, "It's quite simple if you think about it. Absolute truth. You say you believe that two and two is four? It's common knowledge then?"

Captain Blood-Vessel nodded sarcastically in agreement.

"Why?"

Captain BV's expression dropped a bit and he said, "Because it is. Basic pre-school math. Your point?"

Go-God crossed his legs and leaned on an elbow, "My point is; is there anything I could do or say to make you believe that two and two isn't four?"

"No," Captain BV was getting frustrated.

"So, you would call that an absolute truth then?"

"Yes," he answered though a semi-clenched jaw.

"Now, regardless of what you believe; is there anything I could do to make two and two not equal four? To change absolute truth?"

Captain BV flipped his arms in the air a bit, "No. Its math. This is pointless. There you go again. Typical evangelical nonsense. How about you answer my original question?"

Go-God raised his hands, palms up and said, "I just did. How can we both be right? Someone here did their math wrong."

It was at this point that someone off camera must have notified the host that time was almost up. He nodded to the mystery voice and changed gears. He said they were coming to the end of round one and closing arguments were in order. Go-God gave the floor to Captain BV first. He simply restated his previous challenge, "All I want is an answer to my question. Why can't we both be right? Why can't you admit that there are many paths to God? To spirituality? To enlightenment? Why?"

Go-God let the question hang in the air for a moment and then replied, "Absolute truth. Right is right, wrong is wrong. We both agree that two and two equal four. It always has equaled four, and it always will. Nothing can change that. Even if I started my own brand of math that said the sum was five, and I claimed I was being unfairly judged for my belief; if I said that the people who insist that two and two are four are hypocritical bigots, who shove their own brand of autocratic arithmetic down my throat…would it change the truth? Would it change the fact that two and two equal four? No…because truth is truth."

They quickly ran out of time at that point, the credits rolled, and I clicked off the TV and headed for bed. As I lay there half dozing, half stuck in a contemplative whirlwind, some rather salient parallels came to mind. My idea mill was churning.

I've had some pretty strenuous theological wrestling matches over the years with people about the true nature of God, Christianity and "The Church". Some of these people are members of my own family. My parents grew up in "The Church", Catholic and Greek Orthodox to be precise. Our religious conversations almost always inevitably gravitate back to the concept of "The Church". The church, he said with a sigh. The concept of the church has tainted and marred our faith. The Church drives people away. The Church is a judgmental, self-serving institution that adheres to a strict set of rules, regulations and traditions that inevitably end up pushing people like my parents further away from the true message. The simple message of Jesus.

From my experience, and conversations with people about The Church, Jesus, His absolute supreme divinity, His sacrifice for our souls, His (and His alone) selfless act as our creator in the flesh to save us from ourselves--is found in little more than the sermon on Sunday when the New Testament is spoken of.

The teachings of Jesus have been diluted over the millennia. The message of His sacrifice and salvation for our

souls has been overshadowed by centuries of human agendas.
I'm rather positive that Mary, the Earthly mother of Jesus is
not pleased that the Catholics have decided to worship her.
She can't be excited when whole congregations of people, pray
to her for help, protection and salvation instead of her
son…and Lord. Mary sat at the foot of the cross and watched
her son murdered. She watched her God murdered. She wept,
she grieved and she rejoiced when He reappeared. She is one
of us.

I have to believe that she would be thrilled to be
worshipping at the feet of the Lord right next to me. Shoulder
to shoulder. If she can hear the prayers of the Catholics I
always imagine her shrugging with a perplexed look on her face
and pointing to Jesus.

Then I imagine her looking to the hundreds of other
deified men that the Catholic Church has turned into saints
and asking them if it makes them uncomfortable when people
pray to them instead of The Lord God Almighty for
protection, financial success, relief from pain, a cure for an
illness, or forgiveness for sins. "You'll go to hell if you don't
do this," "You'll burn in the fires of Hades if you do that."
Worship this stick because Christ touched it. Revere that cloak
because in the year 182AD Saint Do-Dad wore it when he

preached to the people of Swizzle-Stick so it's a Holy Relic. Condemnation, judgment, rules, regulations and impossible standards.

I hardly think Jesus would approve of anything taking attention away from God the Father and His ultimate sacrifice for us. The moment we start putting our trust in things other than God, Satan's ears perk up. Trust in this amulet to keep you safe while you drive; it has a stenciled picture of St. Christopher on it (Were there cars back in the third century? I digress...). Are you in the middle of the forest and in fear of being attacked by a wild animal...with horns no less?

Then go right ahead and pray to St. Guy of Anderlecht, he'll protect you. And, if you ever have problems with epilepsy, infantile convulsions, mad dogs, rabies, bachelors, convulsive children, laborers, the protection of outbuildings, protection of sheds, protection of stables, sacristans (oh they're bad), sextons (oh no, even worse), or work horses...then he's the man to call as well. A Jack of all trades.

When we take our eyes off of Christ, we lose sight of the goal. When we lose sight of the goal we can stumble off the path. When we fall off of the path we panic and reach for anything to guide us...enter the evil one. "Believe in yourself," he says, "Christ isn't enough."

My point is that all of the extra baggage that has been added by people over the last 2000 years has served to disillusion millions of believers. My parents' reference "The Church" and make a face. I've always wanted a way to get them to see to the heart of faith…behind the layers of muck and years of hurt The Church has slopped on them.

I believe Go-God and Captain Blood Vessel's argument provided me with an idea. As I lay there in bed thinking about 2 and 2 being four and absolute truth being unchanging, a great analogy came to me. Math; absolute truth and how we learn it.

I am not a math person. Numbers never came (or now come) easily to me. It's not that I can't do it, I just can't force myself to think that it's enjoyable. The fact that I don't like it doesn't make it any less true.

So, to math. The arguments I hear over and over again are that "religious" people are so hypocritical. Christians are judgmental, condemning doom preachers. Why would a loving God send people to hell? If a man is born in the middle of the Sahara Desert and never hears the teachings of Jesus, is he going to hell? Where is the justice in that? Why can't there be different paths to heaven? I don't want to believe in a God that is so myopic and single minded. He obviously doesn't love me enough if He is willing to throw me away if I don't proclaim Him my Lord and Master on this side of heaven. If I'm a good person who is nice and loving then God will take me in at the end, He has to.

I feel the answers to these questions lie lost in the midst of my senior year Algebra II class. The question is: If you had an abysmal math teacher, one that didn't know their subject matter, was cruel, judgmental, boring beyond belief and insistent that they were correct even when they were obviously wrong…would that change the absolute truth of math? Would it make math, not true? Somehow flawed? Would 2 and 2 cease to be four if you had a teacher that left a bad taste in your mouth about numbers? The answer is no. Regardless of what humans add to it, do to it, or do in its name…Christianity and the One Almighty God that it is founded on are unchanging.

To presume that a judgmental church body, or a pastor who is unfaithful to his wife, or a child molesting priest, or a doctrine that seems unbiblical represents the movement of faith in Jesus Christ to the world is childish. To presume that an imperfect human being's flawed testimony to the world gives you a "get out of jail free" card to bask in disbelief and to rationalize away your sin is just plain immature. Akin to throwing an "It's not fair" tantrum. It doesn't mean that the message is any less true or sound. It just means that, in a sense, we've had a bad math teacher. I find it interesting that people get upset when a believer speaks about Jesus and judgment.

The opponents of Jesus and His teachings knee-jerkingly sputter off about nobody controlling them, and the fact that they didn't sign up for Christ. They say no one asked them about it, so why should they be held to a set of rules that they don't believe in or agree upon. Again, I find the argument laughable, comparable to an allusion to our own legal system. See if this analogy fits for you.

That viewpoint is comparable to a man saying, "I don't believe in jail therefore I can't go there. I don't believe in court; therefore, it can't sentence me to a jail that I don't believe exists in the first place." Now you look at that person and say, "Well, sorry bud. It really doesn't matter that you say you don't believe in jail, or court, or the police…if you break the law you're still going to go there. Say it's not fair all you want; it is what it is, and that's the truth."

How about, "I don't believe in gravity." You look at them and say, "Well, gravity is real and if you choose to walk off of that cliff you will pinwheel to your death and end your time on Earth as a grease stain at the bottom of this canyon." They simply tell you that you are being a judgmental bigot who insists that everyone follow their brand of truth…then they step off the cliff. The flawed logic is unmistakable. So, the question is why? Why are people so reluctant to let go? What are they getting from holding out? From refusing to accept Jesus' love and forgiveness?

In Romans 6:21, Paul said, "What benefit did you reap at that time from the things that you are now ashamed of? Those things result in death!" That's the issue here. Why are some people so opposed to God? Opposed to the point that the very idea that He exists elicits almost physically violent responses in non-believers. What causes that knee-jerk rebellious reaction?

I've lived in sin. Run from God. As I look back I constantly find myself asking: What benefit did I reap? What do we gain by not following Jesus? What's the payoff? Let's explore that a bit, shall we?

What are the vices…the lusts…desires…the carnal needs that we feed? How about sex? Sex…well, if you choose to sleep around you get just that…sex with random people. No emotional connection, no love, no commitment…just empty physical pleasure. You can also get so much more! STDs…the gifts that keep on giving. Some are annoying, some go away. Some are itchy, some are not. Some make things grow on you, some make things fall off of you (sounds like a demented Dr. Seuss book), and some will kill you (no joke there). You can also get unwanted pregnancies, ruined lives, insatiable lust, and heart break. What real benefit? Fleeting pleasure followed by a lifetime of regret. Great tradeoff.

What else? What is all the fun you'd be missing? Drugs? Alcoholism? Abuse? Anger? Rage? Depression? Anxiety? Sure, sounds like fun. If you're a gambling man (or woman) and you just want to reduce the question of God to a simple mathematical equation listen to what Blaise Pascal had to say about it.

Pascal was a famous mathematician who lived in France during the mid-sixteen hundreds and was responsible for a great number of theories and equations that we still use today. One of these was a postulation that has come to be known as Pascal's Wager or Pascal's Gambit. In it he states that it is a safer bet to believe in God than to choose not to believe based on a simple cost to benefit ratio.

Pascal's Wager	God exists	God does not exist
Living as if God exists	Positive Benefit: Eternal Communion with Jesus and joy in heaven.	No Change
Living as if God does not exist	Negative Consequence: Eternal Separation From God and torment in a hell of your own choosing.	No Change

Based on the possible outcomes, Pascal stated that believing in God is the smarter mathematical choice. If you believe in Him and He exists you "win" the bet so to speak. You get eternal communion with God in heaven. If He doesn't exist then your life goes on status quo, you just believed in something that didn't exist, no harm…no foul. On the other side of the equation, if you choose not to believe in Him and He doesn't exist, then the result is much the same as the first scenario: your life continues on without a hitch. But (and here's the kicker) if you choose to live your life as if The Lord Jesus Christ doesn't exist and He does, you willingly doom yourself to eternal separation from Him. You have chosen to exist apart from Him. The concept that God "sends" people to hell is a misnomer.

The Lord loves us so much that He gives us whatever we want. If we want to spend eternity with Him and we willingly live accordingly He will joyfully oblige and welcome us home. But if we choose to live as if He isn't there and we want no part of Him, He will begrudgingly and with a heavy heart give us our wish. He will let us go to a place where He isn't. If Jesus is light then He agrees to let us go to a place where there is no light, because after all darkness is just the absence of light. There's a saying that goes, the gates of hell are locked from the inside. There is nobody in hell that didn't choose to be there. Based on this, you'd have to be crazy to let it ride on the side of disbelief. You're not betting with last month's paycheck, you're betting with your soul.

I think in the end, it's just about surrendering. Surrendering to God. The pleasures of this world are lies. Fleeting fantasies. Heaven is the truth. Jesus is the truth. Jesus is the truth plain and simple. 2 and 2. Simple as that. Truth is truth no matter how you slice it (or add it up). The next time you get weighed down by the baggage, or condemned by your faith just hold up two fingers on each hand, push them together and see what you get. I'm willing to bet it will be the same every time...barring some horrible woodshop accident.

To answer my original question; "Have two and two always been four?" Yes. Is God who He says He is? Yes. Will anything ever...ever...ever...ever change that fact, no matter how much time passes, how much doctrine is added, how many people are hurt, how many wars are fought in His name, how many children are abused, how many wives are cheated on, how many husbands are neglected, how many bad testimonies are given by weak actions...will it change or cease to be true? No.

As Yankee legend Yogi Berra once said, "It is, what it is."

V. Nicholas Gerasimou

CHAPTER SEVENTEEN

*L*OVE IS...

1 Corinthians 13:4-8

Love is patient, love is kind. It does not envy, it does not boast, it is not proud. It is not rude, it is not self-seeking, it is not easily angered, it keeps no record of wrongs. Love does not delight in evil but rejoices with the truth. It always protects, always trusts, always hopes, always perseveres. Love never fails.

Love. Ah, love. I love you. I LOVE YOU! What some people wouldn't give to hear those words. Hey, I'm one of those people, who am I kidding? I love, love. I love to be loved. I love to love. Love just, is…right?

"Love is what?" you ask. "Well…love…is a many splendid thing?" I respond as I scratch my head looking befuddled. Okay, now you've got me thinking (which can be dangerous). What is love—truly?

The famous Victorian poet Elizabeth Browning thought that "Love doesn't make the world go round; love is what makes the ride worthwhile." Esteemed political psychologist Erich Fromm said, "Love is the only sane and satisfactory answer to the problem of human existence." Poet and author Oliver Wendell Holmes proclaimed that, "Love is the master key that opens the gates of happiness." The actor Robert Mitchum said something that struck a chord in me, he said, "Maybe love is like luck. You have to go all the way to find it."

In reality, love is just a word. Four letters, "L" at the beginning, "E" at the end, "OV" in the middle. The word itself possibly came from the Hebrew word "lehv" (spelled lamed-beyt) which means heart. And if you think about it, the heart has come to symbolize our obsession with love. If you need an example, just take a quick look around at Valentine's Day.

From dawn to dusk, mountains to the valleys, from sea to shining sea, we are inundated with images of the plump, red, two-lobed creation. Television, movies, magazines…I imagine every year around the middle of February there is a small celebration held on the stock market floor hosted by the main shareholders of the Hallmark Corporation. Walk into one of those stores at that time of year and you'll leave with hearts burned into your retinas like you've stared at the sun for a second too long.

We've idealized it, commercialized it, cheapened it and changed it. In reality the heart isn't that attractive. I studied anatomy, physiology and biology in college and let me tell you, from someone who has held a human heart in his hand, it did not make me long to hold the woman I love. It actually looks more like a red, veiny, upside-down pear covered in slime, peritoneum and blood; it just made me want to wash my hands. Ah love…

I think that as a people we've actually lost our way. We've lost the true meaning of love. At times it's just a word to us. I love you. I love it when you do that. I'd love it if you stopped. I love him. I love my wife. I'd love some cream cheese on my bagel. Why is it that I can say that I love the Yankees and my children in the same breath? How can I love Jesus and football at the same time? Well, if you've ever heard the saying "talk is cheap," or "actions speak louder than words," then you might have an idea what I'm getting at.

Let's get down to the heart of the matter (wait for laughing to stop…two, three, and continue) Love is just a word. What matters is the connection the word implies. The true measure of love is what one is willing to do for it, or in some cases not do for it. Would you go without for it? Would you do "it," whatever "it" is? Would you?

In Greek there are five different words for love. Eros, Philia, Storge, Xenia, and Agape. These words have meanings varying from Eros which is the passion and lust one feels for the opposite sex (it's where we get the word erotic from), to affection, to companionship, to the love one feels for a dog. Out of all of the definitions and terms that the Greek gives us, the one word that best fits love for our purpose is Agape. It generally refers to a pure, perfect love. It's God's love. The word agapo is the verbal tense, it is in action, alive…it is doing. It's the love that gives of itself…. actively.

If you really sit back and think about it, talking about love is futile. To be honest I'm kind of a show me, don't tell me guy anyway. I believe if we want to understand what love is, we have to look at what true love has made people do…the actions that it produced. This ($2H2 + O2 \rightarrow 2H2O$ + heat) is the chemical formula for the combustion of hydrogen and oxygen. It's commonly used as rocket fuel.

Now I could have a personal audience with Wernher von Braun, the father of modern rocketry, for hours, and still have a relatively fuzzy concept of what hydrogen and oxygen do when lit on fire. But take me to the NASA launching ground at Cape Canaveral in Florida and let me see 560,000 gallons of super cooled liquid jet fuel exploding at 6000 degrees Fahrenheit, and shoving 165,000-pound space shuttle 300 miles straight up with a 10-story high fire ball that shakes the ground in Georgia…now we're talking. I get it.

So, what does love make people do? What kind of response does true love elicit in the minds and souls of the afflicted? Well, it makes us do crazy things. Crawl out of our comfort zones…maybe crawl is the wrong word--how about leap, sprint, bound…explode? It makes us reevaluate our priorities and change who we are. It makes you stand in the rain, write sappy poetry, and scream their name into the night. It makes their needs paramount to your own. Their TV show is always on and you let them hold the remote.

It makes the thought of sitting alone with them in an empty room seem a more exciting endeavor than skydiving, and when it pours they get the umbrella as you carry the bags. We watch movies we never thought we'd watch, and eat foods we never thought we'd eat (some of us guys don't eat the foods that we really want to eat). We pine, we ponder and we daydream. We would walk through fire, crawl on glass, and watch The Real Housewives of… everywhere. The best part is we would be thrilled to do it. Second thoughts are a thing of the past. Love makes us better people than we would be otherwise. That other person is the catalyst for your dreams.

Love is desire. Mark Twain once said, "Love is the irresistible desire to be irresistibly desired." Without love that statement might be looked upon as desperate or weak, but in love those concepts are null and void. Love makes it okay to fall apart. Love tells you to show all of yourself and not hold anything back…anything, even the things you lie to yourself about. Love lets you let go of who you thought you were and become the person you've always wanted to be.

Love makes you beg, plead and flutter. It brings tears to the most stoic of eyes, and songs to the most reserved lips. It changes your personality. Your pride becomes their pride, which in essence steals its power over you. There is no pride in love. Pride is an illusion, a farce; it's a lie that's pushed on us by the evil one. True love teaches us that the only person that matters is the one who has your heart.

Love gives us hope where there is none. Love makes forgiveness possible. It rights wrongs. It lets you see clearly. Love heals wounds. Love takes the past and washes it clean. It keeps no record of wrongs, which at times goes against every natural reaction of our nature. We like to categorize and catalogue. We tend to try to keep a scorecard of life. Make sure it's even. Love makes it a friendly game where only the good plays are applauded and the misses forgotten. Author and Editor Thomas Mason once said, "The love game is never called off on account of darkness." Well, step into the light. Love makes the future possible, and it makes your past impossible because they aren't in it. Love understands. It makes you capable of an insight that would be otherwise impossible. It makes you want to give up everything you are for them. Love makes love.

Now who am I talking about? The love for your family? Yes. The love for a spouse? Yes. The love for our Lord? Yes. But what is the definition of love? I could sit here and write out the dictionary definition and make deep connections to it in a quirky way but I won't. I think the definition of love is very simple. It's a one-word definition that says more in three syllables than an entire novel by Nicholas Sparks (as moving as they are).

Sacrifice.

Love is sacrifice. Love is giving all of who and what you are for another person without expecting anything back in return. The love of a mother for a newborn child. The love for your spouse of thirty years. The love that the Lord Jesus Christ has for us.

If you want a tangible example of true love look to the Lord. He built the model. He set the bar. Think about it. Over 2000 years ago He looked upon His children and wept. He looked down and His heart broke. His kids were dying apart from Him. They were denying Him, running from Him, they were lost. We were sick, and what parent wouldn't do anything in their power to make their children feel better again...to take away their pain? So, Jesus did the only thing He could do to save us from ourselves. He became one of us.

What is the definition of love? Sacrifice. What is the definition of sacrifice? Like I said, talk is cheap, look at what love made the Creator of the universe do for us. He emptied Himself. He came to us. He left the perfect splendor of heaven to eat bland food, get the flu, skin His knees and eventually suffer and die in our stead. I could go on and on and never scratch the unending cosmic surface of what He gave up for us.

He loved us so much that He decided to take all of the bad that we have done; the evil, the hurt, the wickedness and deceit. He loved us enough to accept all of the wrong that we did, do and will commit and wipe the slate clean. Even more so, He decided that because He loved us so much and so unconditionally that He would even take our place when time came to settle our tabs. The wages of sin are death and The Lord took our place in line.

He did it without regret or a second thought. He suffered. He wallowed in pain. Bleeding, broken, and crushed; He chose to take it on...for us. The Author of life, who thought existence...into...existence, allowed Himself to be abused and tortured by His creations. Why? Why did He do it?

Love.

Sacrifice.

They are one and the same.

He did it so that we could have a chance at happiness: so that we could get a shot at choosing salvation. Love. He wants to spend eternity with us. He gave everything for us. Gave up everything for us. Suffered for us. Died for us. He did so knowing that some of us wouldn't love him back. He did it with the knowledge that some of us would outright deny Him and hate Him. He did it with purpose and power.

That is the key to love. Loving something...someone more than yourself. That is the magical missing piece to the puzzle. Over and over The Lord told us to love. Love one another, love our neighbors as ourselves; He even went as far as to tell us to love our enemies; that's just crazy right? Not when you look at it through His eyes. The secret is love...and love is sacrifice.

At the end of the day it's all about God. It's about relationships. You have to give yourself to Jesus...sacrifice yourself to Him, to truly understand what, and how to do it for somebody else. He is the template. The mold of love. I get it now. I understand. You have to be selfless to get selfless. You have to give to get. You have to sacrifice yourself to live. It's a paradox. Die to live. Christ said that we have to die to ourselves to live for Him. Human marriage is an allusion to the church's relationship to Jesus, just as our gift of ourselves to Him, is the template for how He wants us to love each other.

Mother Teresa once said, "I have found the paradox that if I love until it hurts, then there is no hurt, but only more love." I find that to be truer the more I learn of love. Love is a well that you have to pour yourself into to get yourself out. Only when you draw out your bucket you get much more than you put in. You get forever.

So…love is…

Love is everything. Love is life, forgiveness, patience, grace, mercy, fun, joy, pain, scarring, healing, trust, and faith all rolled into one. Its second chances, third, fourth and fifth chances. Its belief that God works in mysterious ways and He knows what we need before we do. Don't wait. Make the choice. Give yourself away…you'll be surprised at what you get back in return. Trust me…better yet…trust God, He loves you.

CHAPTER EIGHTEEN

*C*orporate Religion vs. Faith: The Pope, The Whole Pope, & Nothing but the Pope.

John 14:6

Jesus answered, "I am the way and the truth and the life. No one comes to the Father except through me.

Where does faith end, and religion start? Is there a difference? Do you need religion to have faith… or, does having a faith cause us to practice a religion?

What came first the chicken or the egg, the faith or the church; or maybe more importantly the relationship with Jesus or the rules and traditions that have been created for us to commune and communicate with Him?

I know that religious division / sects / labeling / denominations / etc, are confusing and frustrating for those who don't have a faith. They're also confusing and frustrating for those of us who do, trust me. Across our nation, for many who associate as Christians or Catholics, religion is now widely looked at as more of a status symbol or a club affiliation than a relationship with The Almighty Creator.

"I am a Catholic." Some say. "We are the original faith, 1.2 Billion strong. Revere me."

"Oh yeah, well IIIIIIII'm a Lutheran. All the taste, half the ceremony. Nail that to your church door and smoke it." Other's retort.

"Well you're both wrong," a third religi-sizer interjects, "I'm a Southern-Baptist, Episcopalian, Charismatic, Faith-Healing, Post-Trib-Christian-Scientist, with a side of hash browns. Get with the times."

Sadly, I fear many are missing the point. Can't see the forest through the trees, or maybe more appropriately, can't see Christ through the stained-glass and incense.

If I had to label myself, I guess I'd say, I'm simply a follower of Jesus Christ, God incarnate whose ultimate once-and-for-all sacrifice made it possible for me to be forgiven for my plethora of continually compounding sins. So you can call me a Christian. I love and believe in Jesus Christ and Him alone. Period.

The reason I'm writing this piece is the fanatic hoopla that has been made over the Pope's recent and historic visit to the United States (*October 2015*).[4] Every news outlet and media service has been focused on his every move. Every facial expression analyzed, every comment debated by political pundits. He dictates the church's stance on important issues. He says what is forgiven, and what is not. The Pope offers blessings and absolves you from your shameful sins. He is, after all, the leader and head of over one-billion Catholics on planet Earth; is he not?

Is he? Is he really?

Well, my view is no. No he is not.

The Pope, the position of the Pope, the institution that has been established by the Catholic Church over the last 1600 or so years has been to elevate Men to glory and power using God as a vehicle. The Pope. His holiness. He is simply a man. Like anyone else. He sins just like everyone else. He has impure thoughts just like anyone else. He needs Jesus's salvation just like anyone else.

He is no closer to God than anyone else. Read the Bible. [F]or all have sinned and fall short of the glory of God.

---

[4] Portions of the following were written in October of 2015 during Pope Francis' visit to the United States

(Romans 3:23) It doesn't say some have sinned. Or most have fallen short. It says, All.

The fact that the "Catholic Church" has established a paradigm wherein a human man is the conduit for a "believer" to communicate with God, receive forgiveness, and "earn" salvation by works, or saying "Hail Marys" or penance, runs contrary to what the simple message of Jesus states.

The Pope is a man, and from what I've seen more of a politician than anything else. He is purporting to speak for God, enacting His will here on Earth. Again, if you read the scripture and listen to the message Jesus preached you will see that the institution of the Pope sounds eerily similar to the Pharisees and Sadducees which Jesus denounced time and time again.

They were the Jewish religious leaders of the time and they stood in between you and God. They were the only way you could communicate with The Lord. They dictated thousands of laws and regulations that you were required to keep under threat of banishment or ridicule, and they elevated themselves above all of their "parishioners" with an air of superiority, advanced social status, expensive and gaudy robes and adornments, and political power.

Thousands of years ago, God gave Moses the Ten-Commandments. Ten laws for the people of Israel to live by. Ten tenants to focus on to stay in God's will. They were simple. Direct. Easy to understand. What happened next was the inevitable desire of man to exert power and control. After the Jewish people crossed the Jordan River and conquered the Holy Land, a system of religious hierarchy was established.

Layers and layers of hypocritic ceremony were heaped together into a Frankenstein's Monster-esque amalgamation of rules that the Hebrew people had to follow to have even a glimmer of a chance to be in God's will. By the time our Lord Jesus was born, the Mitzvot or Jewish Commandments had grown to 613. 613 rules, regulations, stipulations, and restrictions.

They ranged from stringent dietary laws, to sacrificial protocols for the atonement of sins, to pilgrimages, to the economy, to rituals for being ceremonially clean. They were an impossible list for any one person to keep in order. Hence, they all needed religious leaders who were closer to God than they were. Religious leaders who could lead them, guide them, intercede for them hen they fell short.

Those leaders had power. Those leaders had influence and they liked it that way.

Sound familiar?

When Jesus came He made the simple proclamation that He was the Way, the Truth, and the Light. That no one could come to the Father except through Him. There was no more middle-man. No more ceremony. No more hoops to jump through. Jesus came to complete the circle. Somewhere along the way mankind became disconnected from God, Jesus plugged us back in.

The truth is we all have a direct connection to God. A Fastpass to the front of the line. The Batphone if you will. All you need do is simply speak to Him. No buffer. No ceremony. No regulations. No ritual. All you really need to do is read the Bible to see that the majority of what occurs in the Catholic Church today is not found in the Scripture. It is nearly two millennia of men adding rituals, and road-blocks, and qualifiers, and restrictions to a relationship with Jesus to ultimately glorify themselves.

The Catholic Church is a business. A big, powerful, corporate business. A business with scratch in the political arena, and with a vested interest in global economics.

Now those raised in the Catholic Faith will be appalled to read this. I'm sure many will have a visceral / physical reaction to hearing THE VICOR OF CHRIST being questioned. That is simply because for many Catholics, it was how they were raised. Its indoctrination at its finest and I get it. How dare I lambaste your Pope? How dare I blaspheme his holiness?

Therein lies the problem. He is not "His Holiness". He is not holy at all. He is a man. The Lord Jesus is holy. The Lord Jesus is King. The Lord Jesus is in charge. Not Jorge Mario Bergoglio, Pope Francis, the 266th Holy Roman Emperor elected by the papal conclave by means of the College of Cardinals.

The Pope cannot forgive you. Nor can he, for example, forgive women who have had abortions (for only 1 year, act now: 9/01/2015) as he recently stated. The Lord Jesus does that of His own accord. He doesn't need any help... Last time I checked, He was God.

So I guess the point of this is... Anything that takes your eyes off of Jesus and His simple message of love, relationship, and salvation from your sin... Is not Biblical.

Religion vs. Faith and Relationship. Religion says look at me to see how to reach God. Faith simply takes out the middle man (which is what Jesus preached all along). By the way, when Jesus breathed His final completely mortal human breath on the cross, Jerusalem was rocked by a jarring earthquake, "[A]nd the veil of the temple was torn in two from top to bottom. (Mark 15:38)". The separation between man and God was torn asunder. No middle man. Its symbolic.

The Pope is a politician. Does he say nice things that are in a general face-value sense good for the world and the majority of people?

Yes.

Does he kiss children on the forehead and say beautiful blessings over them?

Yes.

Is he probably a very nice person who loves God in his own way?

Maybe.

Is he the holy mouthpiece of Jesus Christ whom we must look to for a connection to God?

No.

CHAPTER NINETEEN

Corporate Religion vs. Faith: An Addendum

The original article was published online and received a good deal of feedback. Some of the feedback was from devout Catholics, some of whom were aghast at what I'd said about the Catholic Church and the Pope. [5]

The following is a response written to one of the messages I received.

I hear everything you said and I applaud your stance and I respect the faith you have. To my original point, "The Pope is merely a man": After reading your viewpoint I keep coming back... to my original point, which then opens the door to a larger discussion on global "religion" and where we are headed as a faith community.

---

[5] www.wordpress.com

The fact of the matter is, Catholics worship men along with God. There is no other way to say it. It is a system that has been indoctrinated into people who originally started off as people who worshiped Jesus Christ and Christ alone, over the last 1600 years or so. It makes sense I guess.

The further you get from the time that Jesus was physically on Earth, the more time there has been for man to take his eyes off of God (Who isn't physically here in a way we can tangibly physically touch) and put our eyes on something we can… men. Its human nature.

Yes, Jesus said to Peter "On this rock I will build my Church," but look at it in context. He said it in 33.AD to a man who literally walked with Jesus. Ate with Him. Spoke with Him. Peter helped establish a faith in God and salvation that Jesus had ordained. There was no faith back then. The word had to be spread. Organically. House to house. City to city. Person to person.

Fast forward 2000 years. Jesus has been in a spiritual state for two millennia and man and his nature for control, glorification, edification, and power has reigned supreme.

"I am the way, the truth, and the life. No one comes to the Father except through Me." John 14:6. There should be no other glory but to God. The Catholic Church and the institution of The Pope have stepped in front of Jesus to take the spotlight.

Catholics worship and pray to men. Saints you call them, but they're just men who did really great things in the past. But I have to believe that when they did these selfless things, some of which got them killed for their faith, they did them out of a love for Jesus Christ, no to be put up on a stained-glass window and prayed to for protection, or prosperity, or a litany of other issues. Catholics pray to Mary the Earthly mother of Jesus. I refer back to John 14:6. Never in the Bible does it say to put your faith in anything other than Jesus Christ. Jesus literally said as much, yet "Hail Mary's" and hundreds of other "Rituals" and "Catholic Traditions" abound.

Much of what you said is rooted in thousands of years of Catholic "Tradition" and "Lore". I've studied the actual history of the Holy Roman Empire and the schism, East and West, Rome, the crusades, the inquisition, the dark ages, on and on. The Catholic Church is an institution that was founded originally in Jesus, wayyyyy back when before Europe existed as we know it, the fall of the Roman Empire, and a lot of other really important historical events yes… but has since become a man-centric, political machine.

The things you stated are true. I'm sure that standing in St. Peter's Basilica is breathtaking and I hope to go there one day, just due to the history and architectural beauty. But the myth that it's built (may or may not be) on Peter's bones, is Catholic tradition and really means nothing in the grand scheme of faith. The Catholic faith reveres relics, "THINGS", places, men, etc. True Christianity and faith in Jesus necessitates only you and God. You could be in the desert, underwater, in a mansion or on the street begging in Bangladesh. We are all the same in the eyes of the Lord.

The knee-jerking almost physical reaction you had to what I said about the Pope, the anger you initially felt, is understandable. Catholics are raised to revere the Pope, Cardinals, Bishops, Priests, Saints, The Virgin Mary, Ceremony, Ritual, and protocol. What I said goes against everything you have been raised to understand as factual. The fact you vehemently defend The Pope and his position, unfortunately kind of proves my point.

The Pope cannot bring the world together. He cannot heal the world because unfortunately this world is destined to end. It's all in Revelation. Our job is to bring as many people to Christ as we can by what we say, what we do, and what we believe.

I guess, to end this, I just have to keep looking back at the Bible. Not pieces, not selections to be interpreted by the church, but Christ's message as a whole. Peter himself said in

Acts, "We must obey God rather than men. 5:29" (I see the irony of what I just did).

V. Nicholas Gerasimou

www.ingramcontent.com/pod-product-compliance
Lightning Source LLC
Chambersburg PA
CBHW072000040426
42447CB00009B/1416